Christmas Through The Ages
BEGINNING WITH THE FIRST NOEL

LONZINE LEE

Christmas Through The Ages

Christmas Through The Ages: Beginning With The First Noel
Copyright © 2024 by Lonzine Lee
Hard cover ISBN: 979-8-9891027-2-3
Paperback ISBN: 979-8-9891027-3-0
E-book ISBN: 979-8-9891027-1-6
Cover design and cover graphic by Salma Lou.
Unless otherwise indicated, all scriptures are taken from The New English Bible, copyright © Cambridge University Press and Oxford University Press 1961, 1970. All rights reserved.
Scriptures marked KJV are taken from the KING JAMES VERSION (KJV): KING JAMES VERSION, public domain.
Scriptures marked AMP are taken from the AMPLIFIED BIBLE (AMPC): Scripture taken from the AMPLIFIED® BIBLE, Copyright © 1954, 1958, 1962, 1964, 1965, 1987 by the Lockman Foundation Used by Permission. www.Lockman.org.
Scriptures marked NAS are taken from the NEW AMERICAN STANDARD 1995 (NAS): Scripture taken from the NEW AMERICAN STANDARD BIBLE®, copyright © 1960, 1962, 1963, 1968, 1971, 1972, 1973, 1975, 1977, 1995 by The Lockman Foundation. Used by permission.
Scripture quotations marked NET are from the New English Translation (NET Bible®), copyright © 1996-2019 by Biblical Studies Press, L.L.C. Used with permission. All rights reserved.
Scriptures marked WMBBE are taken from the World Messianic Bible British Edition, ebible.org, public domain.
A Visit From Saint Nicholas, originally published anonymously in 1823 and later attributed to Clement Clarke Moore, is in the public domain, and is used without permission, as it is freely available for public use and reproduction.

"That Starry Night" illustration was generated using AI technology via Adobe Firefly Generated AI customized based on user-provided specifications. Copyright © August 24, 2024. Licensed to Lonzine Lee. All rights reserved.

"Vintage Christmas Tree" illustration was generated using AI technology via Adobe Firefly Generated AI customized based on user-provided specifications. Copyright © October 21, 2024. Licensed to Lonzine Lee. All rights reserved.

"A Hearthside Christmas Eve" illustration was generated using AI technology via DALL·E by OpenAI, customized based on user-provided specifications. Copyright © November 22, 2024. Licensed to Lonzine Lee. All rights reserved.

"For Unto Us" © Lonzine Lee, 2024. illustration was generated using AI technology via DALL·E by OpenAI, customized based on user-provided specifications. Copyright © November 22, 2024. Licensed to Lonzine Lee. All rights reserved. All rights reserved. This artwork, inspired by Luke 2:8-15, portrays the angel of the Lord appearing to shepherds, surrounded by a heavenly host. This image was created using DALL-E by OpenAI. Unauthorized use, reproduction, or distribution is strictly prohibited without explicit written consent.

"Hark! Hear The Bells" © Lonzine Lee, 2024. illustration was generated using AI technology via DALL·E by OpenAI, customized based on user-provided specifications. Copyright © November 24, 2024. Licensed to Lonzine Lee. All rights reserved. This artwork, inspired by Luke 2:8-15, portrays the angel of the Lord appearing to shepherds, surrounded by a heavenly host. This image was created using DALL-E by OpenAI. Unauthorized use, reproduction, or distribution is strictly prohibited without explicit written consent.

"*Angels In The Sky*" © Lonzine Lee, 2024. illustration was generated using AI technology via DALL·E by OpenAI, customized based on user-provided specifications. Copyright © November 29, 2024. Licensed to Lonzine Lee. All rights reserved. This artwork, inspired by Luke 2:8-15, portrays the angel of the Lord appearing to shepherds, surrounded by a heavenly host. This image was created using DALL-E by OpenAI. Unauthorized use, reproduction, or distribution is strictly prohibited without explicit written consent.

Sound Travels © Lonzine Lee, 2024. illustration was generated using AI technology via DALL·E by OpenAI, customized based on user-provided specifications. Copyright © November 29, 2024. Licensed to Lonzine Lee. All rights reserved. This image is protected by copyright law. No part of this image may be reproduced, distributed, or transmitted in any form or by any means, including photocopying, recording, or other electronic or mechanical methods, without the prior written permission of the copyright holder, except in the case of brief excerpts used for review purposes.

For permissions inquiries, please contact: Lonzine Lee, Dominion Unlimited Publications

Portions of this book contain lyrics from traditional Christmas carols that are in the public domain, including (but not limited to): *The First Noel, Go Tell It On The Mountain, Silent Night, O Come, All Ye Faithful,* and *Joy to the World*. These songs are used without permission, as they are freely available for public use and reproduction.

To My Mother, Dr. Bj Baker
Mommy, thank you for giving us such a love for Christmas. Oh, the memories I have for those lovely Christmas Eves and Mornings.
You always made it fun. You still do. I love you. :)

and

To my Astounding Love! A Global Church Fellowship and Training Center family.
I love you all so much.
His Kingdom has Come.
Blessed Merry Christmas!

Contents

It's Beginning To Look A Lot Like Christmas — 13

The First Noel — 21
Origins of the Christmas Carol

Go, Tell It On The Mountain — 31
The Oral Traditions

A Thrill of Hope — 41
The December 25th Christmas Tradition

Mary, Did You Know? — 55

O Tannenbaum — 67
The Christmas Tree Across Cultures and Time

Not A Creature Was Stirring — 79
The Story of St. Nicholas

Hark! Hear The Bells — 87
The Stories They Tell

I Have A Little Dreidel — 101
A Brief Look At Hanukkah

Troll The Ancient Yuletide Carol — 117
Yule Logs and Mistletoe

'Twas The Birthday of A King — 121
The Best Christmas Story Ever!

O Come, Let Us Adore Him — 151
My Prayer For You

Christmastime is Here! — 157
References & Resources — 159
About the Author — 173
Also by Lonzine Lee — 175

It's Beginning To Look A Lot Like Christmas

From childhood to now, Christmas has always been one of my favorite times of year. I was captivated by the atmosphere of joy, celebration, singing, and the beautiful lights that twinkled on almost all of the houses around town. Even then, the Santa Claus story did not ring true. And yes, I knew the day to be a celebration of the Lord Jesus' birthday.

I lived with my grandmother during the elementary school part of my childhood. When Christmas time came along, my grandmother would put up an aluminum branch tree in front of the living room window. As I grew older, I remember pulling each silver branch out of a brown paper sheath, which we would then fit into the holes drilled into the central pole. The final result was a shiny tree decorated with glossy blue ornaments; enhanced by the color wheel that changed the branches from red to blue to green to gold. I still smile when thinking about those days.

I remember sitting in the darkened living room on those long-ago December evenings. Watching the rotating wheel cast its colors on the tree and the walls was peaceful and magical. This was Christmas.

In later years, when I went to live with my mom, the silver branches were replaced with a big white-flocked living tree. The ornaments varied by color and size. And even though we adorned the tree with garland and strings of lights, we still had the multicolor light wheel.

My childhood Christmases are a treasure trove of memories. Our family traditions included putting up our tree, riding around town looking at all the decorated houses, the annual Rankin/Bass programs, oohs and aahs over gifts, and visiting with family over our meal—followed by the inevitable letdown that it would all soon be over. Dinner and dessert always tasted better on my grandmother's gold and white china plates, reserved for these special occasions.

The First Noel was my initial favorite, followed later by lots of others. There have been so many songs introduced over the years, of course, but these were days when I first learned to sing from my heart and become part of the joy, beauty, and fun of Christmas.

♪The first noel, the angels did say, was to certain poor shepherds in fields where they lay.

Up on a housetop, reindeer fall. Down through the chimney comes Santa Claus...

Silent night, holy night. All is calm. All is bright.

It came upon a midnight clear, the glorious song of old...

Said the night wind to the little lamb, "Do you hear what I hear?"

O little town of Bethlehem, how still we see thee lie…

Away in a manger, no crib for a bed. The little Lord Jesus lay down His sweet head.

Joy to the world, the Lord has come! Let earth receive her King!

O come, let us adore Him. O come let us adore Him. O come let us adore Him, Christ the Lord.

Angels we have heard on high, sweetly singing over the plain.

Let's go for a sleigh ride, a wonderful sleigh ride!

Just hear those sleigh bells jingling, ring-ting, tingling too. C'mon, it's lovely weather for a sleigh ride together with you.

City sidewalks, busy sidewalks, dressed in holiday cheer. In the air is the feeling of Christmas.

Hark hear the bells, sweet silver bells. All seem

to say, throw cares away...

O holy night, the stars are brightly shining. It is the night of our dear Savior's birth. Long lay the world, in sin and error, pining. Till He appeared, and the soul felt its worth.

Born is the King of Israel.

THERE ARE OTHER FUN, JOYOUS, sacred, silly, nostalgic, worshipful, and beautiful types of celebratory songs, many more than what I sampled above. Carols, both lyrical and instrumental, chants, folk songs, choir arrangements and solos. The music is sung accapela and with the accompaniment of instruments of brass, string, percussion, and wind. And then there are the bells. Especially the bells.

For me, Christmas bells became synonymous to Christmas joy. And that still holds true today. Maybe you can guess my favorite song. 😎

Regardless of the actual date, the annals of history testify that there is a significant day in time when the words held true:

Jesus Christ is born!

Blessed Merry Christmas!

 *For a boy has been born for us, a son given to us to bear the symbol of dominion on his shoulder; and he shall be called in purpose wonderful, in battle God-like, Father for all time, Prince of peace. Great shall the dominion be, and boundless the peace bestowed on David's throne and on his kingdom, to establish it and sustain it with justice and righteousness from now and for evermore..."* Isaiah 9:6 NET

The First Noel

ORIGINS OF THE CHRISTMAS CAROL

Theologians in the early centuries of Christianity recognized that the nature of Christ's Incarnation was a moment that marked the renewal of creation itself. But how was it to be commemorated? Tracing the origin of the songs referred to as "Christmas Carols" is an interesting exploration into one way that the birth of the Christ child was first celebrated.

Historically, the very first "Cristes maesse" or "Christ's mass"[1] carol is attributed to St. Hilary of Poitiers (France) in the fourth century (AD 368). The song, *Jesus Refulsit Omnium* [Jesus, Light of All the Nations] was written and sung in Latin and as a Gregorian chant. However, some scholars consider Italy to be the birthplace of the first true Christmas carol. St.

Francis of Assisi is regarded as the first to introduce joyous carols, or at least contribute to the idea of truly celebrating the birth of Christ. *Canticle of the Sun (Laudes Creaturarum* in Italian).

But the earliest carol of my youth is *The First Noel*.

THE ORIGIN AND HISTORY OF Christmas carols meant nothing to me when I was in elementary school. Music time was a part of our regular curriculum, but it was during a Christmas season that a certain holiday recording was played for us. I seem to recall it being my fourth-grade classroom. As the introductory chords were played, I was instantly captured by the first line.

We first listened to learn, then would sing along until we could sing the song acapella. This was all in preparation for a later performance. Periodically, our school would hold mass assemblies where each grade level would perform a song or a skit in the cafeteria/gym. And so it is, that my heart was thrilled from the first time we sang in the assembly,

> 🎵 *The First Noel, the angels did say, was to certain poor shepherds in fields where they lay…* 🎶

The embers of my soul were stirred, and the first flame of musical passion ignited.

> 🎵 *Noel. Noel. Noel. Noel. Born is the King of Israel.* 🎶

This melody still strikes the chords of my being. As I questioned the why of this, the answer is simple. This is the song that first pointed me to my King. After all these years, I still find it beautiful, and my heart continues to resonate with the imagery and expressions of joy and love released into the earth for the birth of the Lord Jesus Christ.

THE FIRST NOEL IS SAID TO HAVE originated in Cornwall, South West England, sometime during the 13th or 14th century, also known as the Proto-Renaissance period. Still other accounts attribute its origin to the 15th or 16th century, with its earliest forms likely emerging from oral traditions among Cornish villagers and shepherds, who would sing communal songs during Christmas festivities. However, the first English version of the song to be published was in 1823 by William Sandys in *Carols Ancient and Modern.*

There are roughly nine different stanzas or verse that have been down the centuries. And the carol even has a few alternate titles and English spellings:

> *For Christmas Day In The Morning*
> *The First Noel*
> *The First Nowel*
> *A Carol For The Epiphany*

Although this carol is firmly associated with English traditions, some claim that its origins lie in France. The French text, *Le Premier Noël,* shares the same name origin but narrates a different nativity story. The word "Noel" comes from the Old French *nuel,* which is derived from the Latin adjective *natalis*, meaning "of birth" or "relating to birth."

Theologically, there are many objections to the veracity of some of the stanzas, so it is not on everyone's playlist. Let's just say the idea of shepherds in the field on a cold winter's night when it most likely would have been springtime—historical and cultural evidence suggests that sheep were grazed in open fields during the warmer spring months. Additionally, the carol commingles the shepherds' visit with the Magi's arrival. According to the Gospel of Matthew, that visit occurred much later, in a different location. These a just a couple of the lyrical liberties that give rise to criticism, and explains why the song still draws criticism from biblical scholars.

I imagine the writers of the song were thinking about their own winter nights and exercised their creative genius for the sake of poetic imagery. Then again, it might not have been that deep. After all, they were recounting a story in a manner common in oral traditions, where accuracy often gives way to narrative appeal.

. . .

Regardless, this beautiful carol with the joyous melody recounts what we call the nativity story with vivid imagery, including angels announcing the event, shepherds witnessing the star, and the eventual journey to see the truth of what they heard with their own eyes - the heralded birth of the newborn King.

English composer and organist Sir John Stainer, was known as a leading early musicologist, as well as being a key figure in preserving traditional carols. He is credited with harmonizing the modern melody for *The First Noel* in 1871, and his version is the most commonly known melody today. Stainer's arrangement, is the one that is included in the collection *Christmas Carols, New and Old*. It reflects the transition from oral tradition to structured, harmonized carols for congregational singing.

This song has been covered many times over the centuries, with varying lyrics, depending upon the artists and the nation doing the singing. It is still quite popular with choirs and recording artists, plus it has the verve and versatility to be adapted to numerous genres, including jazz, pop, country, rap, and R&B.

And like many other holiday favorites, *The First Noel is* a perfect example of oral traditions, as it was handed down from one generation to another, from its origins in the community sings of rural England to today, its a beautiful illustration of how stories and music are sustained over generations, right down to their core themes of hope, joy, and celebration.[2]

The Night of The First Noel

> "Now there were in the same country shepherds living out in the fields, keeping watch over their flock by night. And behold, an angel of the Lord stood before them, and the glory of the Lord shone around them, and they were greatly afraid."
>
> — LUKE 2:8-9 NKJV

As I read Luke's account of the shepherds on the night they heard about the birth of a king, I wonder what it was like for them to experience such an over the top event.

Imagine, there they are in the field, going through the motions of an ordinary night watching over the sheep. I have lots of little questions that lead to a bigger one. Who owned the sheep? Were they temple-owned, or did they belong to wealthy landowners? The thing about shepherds is that they are tough and seasoned in their abilities not only to guard sheep, but to care for their needs and protection.

Shepherding is year-long, not seasonal, so they had to know how to fight off predators, live among the sheep they cared for, watch over the birthing of new lambs, and make sure the temple-bred sheep were blemish free. Like farmers, ranchers, fishermen, truckers, and other tradespeople in our society that contribute to our daily lives, shepherds contributed to their local economy, providing wool, meat, and milk. Their work even supported religious practices. Remember, sheep were one of the animals used in sacrificial offerings.

> Then the angel said to them, "Do not be afraid, for behold, I bring you good tidings of great joy which will be to

all people. For there is born to you this day in the city of David a Savior, who is Christ the Lord. And this *will be* the sign to you: You will find a Babe wrapped in swaddling cloths, lying in a manger." And suddenly there was with the angel a multitude of the heavenly host praising God and saying: 'Glory to God in the highest, And on earth peace, goodwill toward men!'"

— LUKE 2:10-14 NKJV

Shepherds watching over the sheep carried a staff, a rod, and a sling to guide and defend the flocks. We read about that in Psalm 23. But not one of their tools would be able to protect them from an angelic appearance. Think about it. There they are in the night watch, and suddenly the skies light up like it's daytime. A massive heavenly messenger appears and speaks to them, telling them not to be afraid. I don't think it worked.

Of course they were afraid. Did they fall to their knees in reverence, awe, and fear? I think so. But all the while, I believe they still watched over their sheep, which I believe were paying attention as the angel proclaimed the news. The shepherds were the first to receive the message from Heaven. There had been a *noel*, a birth unlike any other. That very day, in the city of David, a king had been born; and it was to these that watched over the sheep, that the arrival of the King of all kings, the one that would be known both as The Lamb of God and The Good Shepherd was announced. To them had been given the oral tradition story fit for all ages to come.

Yes, this truly was the night of *The First Noel*.

Go, Tell It On The Mountain

THE ORAL TRADITIONS

Long before written records existed, oral traditions were a vital means of preserving cultural identity, knowledge, customs, health remedies, recipes, child-rearing, genealogies, and historical narratives across generations.

People talked to one another—the elders passed down family traditions, beliefs, philosophies, and skillsets to the younger generation. In early hunter-gatherer and agricultural societies, myths, genealogies, and rituals were transmitted orally, a form of communication distinct from the ancient scrolls, tablets, and hieroglyphics that continue to be discovered today.

> *One* generation passes away, and *another* generation comes; but the earth abides forever...That which has been *is* what will be, That which *is* done is what will be done, And *there is* nothing new under the sun. Is there anything of which it may be said, See, this *is* new"? It has already been in ancient times before us. *There is* no remembrance of former *things,* Nor will there be any remembrance of *things* that are to come By *those* who will come after.[1]

THEOLOGIANS REFER TO ORAL CUSTOM as the passing down of a code of conduct from the Torah, which encompasses every aspect of life, including the rituals, worship practices, dietary laws, Sabbath and festival observations, marital relations, agricultural practices, civil claims and damages.[2] These oral traditions were accompanied by communal rituals, music, and mnemonic devices—such as patterns of letters, ideas, or sounds—to ensure a degree of accuracy and continuity. In that sense, we could say that the oral preservation of the teachings of Jesus and traditions upheld in the early

Church likely began with His disciples—preceding the transcription of the gospels and the letters.[3]

Now, as it pertains to the passing down of Christmas carols within a community, we will look at the oral traditions of storytelling. It's fun to explore the artistic facet of oral traditions—which relied on narrative performance to preserve and share knowledge, myths, and histories.

DURING THE MEDIEVAL AGES, traveling orators, poets, and storytellers—known as minstrels, jongleurs, troubadours, scops, bards, skalds, and goliards—contributed greatly to the woven tapestry of human history, relaying news through words and melodies. Songs, comprised of words that paint vivid pictures, evoke memories, causing us to move our feet and hands, to nod or throw back our heads in expressions of pure joy, dance, or other expressions of movement.

Thus, oral traditions have entered our hearts, minds, emotions, and lifestyles. To a great degree, they have even affected our cultures and our view of own lives. Musical stories, using techniques such as repetition, rhythm, song, and vivid imagery captivate listeners and ensure the tale is passed down accurately, or as best as the messenger can remember. Oral traditions reflect our past and present-day cultural values, societal norms, and collective memory of community, adapting over time as they are continually retold.

Just imagine, from one generation to another, songs evolving from earlier practices of communal singing and storytelling have continued to be passed down. But it wasn't just the songs and stories, it was also the knowledge and insights of historical cultural connections—the vibrancy of people we are connected to—ancestry we learn about through their stories. Even the joy or emotion that these lyrical stories communicate serve as a thread that weaves us into the societal ways and mores of a different, yet same kind of people from times past.

As we will see, many of the songs we refer to as classic, traditional, or even sacred Christmas carols emerged from pagan festivals and practices. From times when winter solstice celebrations included songs about nature and life cycles. The word "*carol*" originally referred to a circle or lively dance accompanied by singing, dating back to medieval Europe. Isn't that something? Oral tradition could romantically be viewed as a continual dance, a form of movement that transcends generations.

And over the centuries, the Christian church adapted these traditions to convey biblical narratives and messages of Christ's birth. From the ancient near east to the medieval middle ages, the time of the Renaissance, and beyond to these contemporary days, patterns of festivity, celebratory music, miracle plays, and dance conjoin with the human spirit from different nations to tell the stories of our lifetimes.

Our joys, struggles, trials, tribulations, heartaches, and celebrations all end up in stories. Humanity's compelling need to **go and tell somebody** continues to be expressed in spoken and melodic tradition to spread the news, *"as it was said in days of old."*

The Story of Go Tell It On The Mountain

Among the rich tapestry of songs preserved through oral traditions is *Go Tell It On The Mountain*. Often performed at Christmas, this Negro Spiritual (as it was styled), carries the biblical message of the shepherds spreading the news of Christ's birth found in Luke 2:8–20.

> *"Go, tell it on the mountain, over the hills and everywhere.*
>
> *Go, tell it on the mountain, that Jesus Christ is born."*

These words fit the classic oral storytelling tradition to, *"Go tell somebody!"* This particular song is not just a form of worship, but it is the cry of heraldry and hope — *I have an announcement to make!*—a story to tell that transcends every human experience. This can also be considered as a tool for teaching, evangelism, and building a community of people that choose to push through opposition to attain the beauty on the other side of pain.

One thing that causes this carol to stand separate from some of the others is that it does not have its roots in paganism. Instead, the origin of *Go Tell It On The Mountain* comes from the slave quarters on plantations in the United States of America. It's a beautiful testimony to realize that this is one of a number of songs that was retrieved from oral transmission, and was actually written down.

Beyond saying that it comes from enslaved Blacks in the 1800s, the attribution of authorship for the origins of *Go Tell It On The Mountain* is given to John Wesley Work, Jr. (August 6, 1871 - September 7, 1925). Mr. Work was a musicologist, choral director, songwriter, educationalist, singer, and a passionate collector of folk songs and spirituals. I think he was also a storykeeper, as he is somewhat known as the first Black collector of Negro spirituals, songs that were seldom recorded on paper, just passed down orally, from plantation to plantation. In the 1907 publication *New Jubilee Songs and Folk Songs of the American Negro*, he ensured the preservation of *Go Tell It On The Mountain*.[4]

As the son of a church choir director, Work was quite the educated man, earning a Master's in

Latin, he also taught Latin and Greek, but his first love was music. Thanks to John Work, it made its way from the plantation fields to concert halls to recording studios and across the world.

How did the words get from one plantation to another? They traveled with the slaves, in the tradition of people of all nations. Life is hard, we're treated unfairly, sometimes it feels like there is no hope for change. Regardless, keep telling people everywhere you go, *Jesus Christ is born.*

Again, that's the power of the gospel of the Kingdom—wherever it goes, so goes another message of hope and redemption through the birth of a King.

Its journey from the oral tradition of a people in captivity to written hymn mirrors the evolution and power of many spirituals and folk songs. Again, the resilience of the human spirit shines through the vilest of circumstances, showcasing the power of releasing the right words in every season. This story had to be preserved, because the people chose to keep telling it.

When you realize how much the story of John Wesley Work, Jr. is intertwined with this song, I hope you find it of interest to study more about him. This carol carries a story and legacy, and the worship all belongs to Jesus. You'll find a number of recommended readings, including a few recorded versions in the **References & Resources** at the end of the book.[5]

Go Tell It On The Mountain
John Wesley Work, Jr., 1907

Refrain:
Go, tell it on the mountain,
Over the hills and everywhere
Go, tell it on the mountain,
That Jesus Christ is born.

While shepherds kept their watching
Over silent flocks by night
Behold throughout the heavens
There shone a holy light.
Refrain
The shepherds feared and trembled,
When lo! Above the earth,
Rang out the angels chorus
That hailed the Savior's birth.
Refrain
Down in a lowly manger
The humble Christ was born
And God sent us salvation
That blessed Christmas morn.
Go, tell it on the mountain,
Over the hills and everywhere
Go, tell it on the mountain,
That Jesus Christ is born.

A Thrill of Hope

THE DECEMBER 25TH CHRISTMAS TRADITION

> *To every thing there is a season, and a time to every purpose under the heaven: A time to be born..."*

Since the Bible does not provide us with the exact date of Jesus' birth, did you ever wonder why we observe the advent of Christ when we do? The reason for our traditional celebration has both theological and historical roots which you may consider to be of interest.

It is said that the decision to celebrate the birth of Christ on December 25 derived from theological reflection and symbolic meaning. The theologians and historians believed to have chosen this date did so for a combination of reasons.

The birth of Jesus not only marked the beginning of His earthly life but also the renewal of creation itself. Early theologians such as Tertullian, Hippolytus of Rome, John Chrysostom, and Augustine of Hippo recognized the miracle of Christ's incarnation—God taking on the form of humanity—as a momentous event.

WHERE DID THEY GET THE IDEA TO commemorate the birth of the most significant person ever to enter into humanity? Imagine the dialogues and questions they must have had with themselves, possibly with the Holy Spirit, and with others. *How do we celebrate this? What can we do to commemorate His life? How do we honor and show our God how much His gift matters to us?*

Early Theologians on the Nativity

Tertullian (c. 150–240 CE): Although he did not explicitly date the birth of Christ, *he was one of the earliest Christian theologians who wrote about the significance of the Incarnation.* Tertullian was the first theologian to write in

Latin, and is attributed to be the one that coined the phrase, the Trinity, in referring to the Godhead. His writings on the theological importance emphasize the reality of Christ's entry in the world and His Incarnation, laying the foundation for later discussions on Christ's birth.[1]

HIPPOLYTUS OF ROME (C. 170–235 AD): Hippolytus is another of the first to propose December 25 as the date of Christ's birth, in his *Commentary on Daniel*, he links it to the creation and symbolism of light. In the early third century, he is said to have believed that the very timing of Jesus' entrance into the world was divinely ordained and designed to align with the darkest days of the year, when the light of the sun began to return after the winter solstice. In this wise, Christ, the "light of the world," was made a symbol of the world's redemption and renewal.[2]

He is one of the earliest theologians to comment extensively on Scripture, especially the Old Testament. He is also known by some for his opposition to certain Roman bishops, leading to him being considered the first antipope. And yet, he was reconciled to the Church before his martyrdom and is celebrated as a saint. His works provide valuable insight into early Christian liturgy and theology.

Hippolytus appears to have tied December 25 to theological typology, seeing the date as the culmination of God's creative and redemptive plan. He believed Christ's birth coincided with the renewal of creation, aligning with early Christian symbolic interpretations of the calendar.

In fact, he actually mentions the date of December 25 in his *Commentary on Daniel*. In Book 4, Section 23.3, he states: *"For the first advent of our Lord in the flesh, when he was born in Bethlehem, was December 25th."*[3]

His work *Apostolic Tradition* provides early evidence of liturgical practices that would evolve into Christian celebrations, including feasts honoring Christ's life and ministry.

JOHN CHRYSOSTOM (C. 347–407 AD): WAS a bishop and theologian born in Antioch (modern-day Turkey). As the Archbishop of Constantinople, he was known for his golden-mouthed oratory skills, fiery sermons and teachings. Chrysostom defended the December 25 date by way of connections. He linked this date to theological and scriptural traditions, arguing that it marked the Incarnation and fulfillment of Old Testament prophecies, and placed March 25 as the date of the Annunciation—when the angel Gabriel visited Mary—and Christ's birth exactly nine months later. The objective was not just to establish a calendar; but also to affirm that the mystery of the Incarnation touched every part of the universe from time itself to the human heart.

As a bishop in Constantinople, he popularized and formalized the celebration of Christmas in the Eastern Church, helping to unify its observance across Christian communities.

The quotations and excerpts from his *Homily on the Date of Christmas* provide insight into Chrysostom's view of Christ's nativity as a transformative event.

"The Ancient of Days has become an infant. He

who sits upon the sublime and heavenly throne, now lies in a manger."

"What shall I say! And how shall I describe this birth to you? For this wonder fills me with astonishment. The Ancient of Days has become an infant. He who sits upon the sublime and heavenly throne, now lies in a manger. And he who cannot be touched, who is simple, without complexity, and incorporeal, now lies subject to the hands of men."

"For this He assumed my body, that I may become capable of His Word; taking my flesh, He gives me His spirit; and so He bestowing and I receiving, He prepares for me the treasure of life."

"Come, then, let us observe the Feast. Truly wondrous is the whole chronicle of the Nativity. For this day the ancient slavery is ended, the devil confounded, the demons take to flight, the power of death is broken, paradise is unlocked, the curse is taken away, sin is removed from us, error is driven out, truth has been brought back."[4]

AUGUSTINE OF HIPPO (354–430 AD): Augustine of Hippo, also known as Saint Augustine, was a prominent theologian, philosopher, and bishop in the early Christian Church, regarded as one of the most important Church Fathers in both Catholicism and Protestantism. Born in Thagaste (modern-day Algeria), Augustine lived during the late Roman Empire.

In the pagan world, December 25 was known as the *Dies Natalis Solis Invicti (Birthday of the Unconquered Sun)*. According to some, Jesus was often depicted in the early Church as *Sol Invictus, the "Unconquered Sun."*

It is in his *Sermon 190: On the Feast of the Nativity* that Augustine stirs our souls with his reflections on the significance of celebrating Christ's birth. He is speaking of the birth of the true Son, in response to those that observed *Dies Natalis Solis Invicti (Birthday of the Unconquered Sun)*, stating: **"Let us celebrate this day as a feast not for the sake of this sun, which is seen by both good and bad, but for the sake of Him who made the sun."**

This sermon is a must read — the expressed passion this man of God pours out is convicting today. His desire for followers of the sun to worship the Son of God is, as the youth of today would say, FIRE! 🔥

It is true that none of these theologians directly initiated the December 25 celebration, however, their writings, liturgical contributions, and theological reflections were pivotal in shaping early Christian understanding of the Nativity, just as the way they all emphasized the Incarnation as central to Christian faith gave theological weight to the celebration of Christ's birth.

John Chrysostom played the most active role in advocating for December 25, whereas Augustine and Hippolytus provided the theological and symbolic framework that supported its observance. Together, their influence cemented the significance of Christmas in the Christian liturgical calendar.

As we close out this chapter, I want to review a few of the ways in which the paganistic aspect of winter was challenged with the theological interpretation of Christ's birth.

Association with Light and the Winter Solstice: Early Christians regarded the winter solstice (December 21 or 22) as the time of celebrating Christ's birth to emphasize the triumph of the Light of the World (Christ) over sin and death (darkness). This is interesting because, to the Roman culture, the winter solstice viewed it as the time when days began to lengthen, symbolizing the return of [lesser] light.

Connection with Creation and New Beginnings: The belief by some theologians that Jesus' conception took place on March 25, the same date as the Annunciation (when the angel Gabriel announced to Mary that she would conceive Jesus), placed His birth nine months later, on December 25. They connected this idea of Jesus' birth to creation and new beginnings, in alignment with the theological concept of Jesus as the "new or second Adam" who brings redemption.

Roman Festival of Sol Invictus: December 25 was already a day of celebration among the Romans, also being the date of the Roman festival of *Sol Invictus ("Unconquered Sun")*. This was the day they celebrated the sun god and the return of longer days after the solstice. The idea has often been attributed to historians suggesting that the celebration of Christ's birth on this date was meant to offer an alternative to the pagan festival, by giving the name and identity of Christ as the true "Sun of Righteousness." [5]

Christianization of Pagan Holidays: With the expansion of Christianity through the Roman Empire, Church leaders sometimes chose to reframe existing pagan celebrations with Christian meanings. The objective was to make it easier for converts to adopt Christian practices because they were similar, but different. By turning December 25 into a celebration of Jesus' birth, they could "Christianize" the popular pagan celebrations of the time.

Formal Acceptance of December 25 As The Birthday of Jesus Christ

Honestly, the quest for understanding can be a lot of fun. The earliest record of December 25 being celebrated as the birth of Christ dates to the mid-fourth century. A Roman almanac mentions a festival of the "Nativity of Christ" on the date of December 25. Pope Julius I is traditionally credited with formalizing the 25th of December as the official date for celebrating Christ's birth.

Now, most of us are not familiar with the **Chronograph of 354**, also known as the **Calendar of Filocalus**. This was a 4th-century illuminated manuscript initially created in 354 C.E. for a wealthy Roman Christian named Valentinus, by one Furius Dionysius Filocalus.

One of the most interesting aspects of this almanac is that it provides the earliest known reference to December 25 as the date of Jesus Christ's birth. The calendar entry states, "**VIII kal. Ian. natus Christus in Betleem Iudeae,**" which translates to "*December 25, Christ was born in Bethlehem of Judea.*" [6]

This reference is significant in answering our original question: Why do we celebrate Christmas on December 25?

To summarize: December 25 was chosen for the celebration of Christ's birth due to 1) theological symbolism related to light and redemption, 2) its alignment with existing Roman festivals, and the desire to offer a Christian alternative to pagan celebrations.

And that is how this date became the accepted and traditional time for commemorating the Nativity of Jesus.

But is it really His birthday? Ah, that's another story altogether.

For now, let's just take note that the writings and reflections of these early theologians laid the foundation for a tradition that has endured for centuries. Think about it—the celebration of Christ's birth is not merely a historical event, but the rebirth in the world itself—a moment when time, creation, and eternity converged in the person of Jesus.[7]

Mary, Did You Know?

And in the sixth month the angel Gabriel was sent from God unto a city of Galilee, named Nazareth, To a virgin espoused to a man whose name was Joseph, of the house of David; and the virgin's name was Mary. And the angel came in unto her, and said,

> Hail, thou that art highly favoured, the Lord is with thee: blessed art thou among women.

And when she saw him, she was troubled at his saying, and cast in her mind what manner of salutation this should be. And the angel said unto her,

> FEAR NOT, MARY: FOR THOU HAST FOUND FAVOUR WITH GOD. AND, BEHOLD, THOU SHALT CONCEIVE IN THY WOMB, AND BRING FORTH A SON, AND SHALT CALL HIS NAME JESUS. HE SHALL BE GREAT, AND SHALL BE CALLED THE SON OF THE HIGHEST: AND THE LORD GOD SHALL GIVE UNTO HIM THE THRONE OF HIS FATHER DAVID: AND HE SHALL REIGN OVER THE HOUSE OF JACOB FOR EVER; AND OF HIS KINGDOM THERE SHALL BE NO END.

Then said Mary unto the angel,

> How shall this be, seeing I know not a man?

And the angel answered and said unto her,

> THE HOLY GHOST SHALL COME UPON THEE, AND THE POWER OF THE HIGHEST SHALL OVERSHADOW THEE: THEREFORE ALSO THAT HOLY

THING WHICH SHALL BE BORN OF THEE SHALL BE CALLED THE SON OF GOD. AND, BEHOLD, THY COUSIN ELISABETH, SHE HATH ALSO CONCEIVED A SON IN HER OLD AGE: AND THIS IS THE SIXTH MONTH WITH HER, WHO WAS CALLED BARREN. FOR WITH GOD NOTHING SHALL BE IMPOSSIBLE.

And Mary said,

> Behold the handmaid of the Lord; be it unto me according to thy word.

And the angel departed from her.

AND MARY AROSE IN THOSE DAYS, AND went into the hill country with haste, into a city of Juda; And entered into the house of Zacharias, and saluted Elisabeth. And it came to pass, that, when Elisabeth heard the salutation of Mary, the babe leaped in her womb; and Elisabeth was filled with the Holy

Ghost: And she spake out with a loud voice, and said,

> Blessed art thou among women, and blessed is the fruit of thy womb. And whence is this to me, that the mother of my Lord should come to me? For, lo, as soon as the voice of thy salutation sounded in mine ears, the babe leaped in my womb for joy. And blessed is she that believed: for there shall be a performance of those things which were told her from the Lord.

And Mary said,

> My soul doth magnify the Lord, And my spirit hath rejoiced in God my Saviour. For he hath regarded the low estate of his handmaiden: for, behold, from henceforth all generations shall call me blessed. For he that is mighty hath done to me great things; and holy is his name. And his mercy is on them that fear him from generation to generation. He hath shewed strength with his arm; he hath scattered the proud in the imagination of their hearts. He hath put down the mighty from

their seats, and exalted them of low degree. He hath filled the hungry with good things; and the rich he hath sent empty away. He hath holpen his servant Israel, in remembrance of his mercy; As he spake to our fathers, to Abraham, and to his seed for ever.

And Mary abode with her about three months, and returned to her own house.

AND IT CAME TO PASS IN THOSE DAYS, that there went out a decree from Caesar Augustus, that all the world should be taxed. (And this taxing was first made when Cyrenius was governor of Syria.) And all went to be taxed, every one into his own city. And Joseph also went up from Galilee, out of the city of Nazareth, into Judaea, unto the city of David, which is called Bethlehem; (because he was of the house and lineage of David:) To be taxed with Mary his espoused wife, being great with child.

And so it was, that, while they were there, the days were accomplished that she should be delivered. And she brought forth her firstborn son, and wrapped him in swaddling clothes, and laid him in a manger; because there was no room for them in the inn.

And there were in the same country shepherds abiding in the field, keeping watch over their flock by night. And, lo, the angel of the Lord came upon them, and the glory of the Lord shone round about them: and they were sore afraid. And the angel said unto them,

> Fear not: for, behold, I bring you good tidings of great joy, which shall be to all people. For unto you is born this day in the city of David a Saviour, which is Christ the Lord. And this shall be a sign unto you; Ye shall find the babe wrapped in swaddling clothes, lying in a manger.

And suddenly there was with the angel a

multitude of the heavenly host praising God, and saying,

> **GLORY TO GOD IN THE HIGHEST, AND ON EARTH PEACE, GOOD WILL TOWARD MEN.**

And it came to pass, as the angels were gone away from them into heaven, the shepherds said one to another,

> Let us now go even unto Bethlehem, and see this thing which is come to pass, which the Lord hath made known unto us.

And they came with haste, and found Mary, and Joseph, and the babe lying in a manger. And when they had seen it, they made known abroad the saying which was told them concerning this child. And all they that heard it wondered at those things which were told them by the shepherds. But Mary kept all these things, and pondered them in her heart.

> *But Mary kept all these things, and pondered them in her heart.*

According to the *Theological Dictionary of the New Testament*, the Greek word used to describe Mary's pondering of events in her heart is *Symballō* (συμβάλλω). It is used in the New Testament to describe the act of pondering or considering something deeply, often in a reflective or meditative manner. *Symballō* can also refer to the act of conferring or discussing with others, as well as encountering or meeting.

WORD STUDY: Symballō[1] translates the Greek participle "συμβάλλουσα" (symballousa), derived from the verb "συμβάλλω" (symballō). This verb combines "σύν" (syn, meaning "together") and "βάλλω" (ballō, meaning "to throw"), conveying the idea of bringing together or considering collectively.

In this context, it signifies Mary's deep reflection and contemplation on the events surrounding Jesus' birth.

Rick Renner, in his book, *Sparkling Gems from the Greek, Volume 1* explains that *symballō* conveys the idea of throwing things together or considering them in one's mind, indicating a deep, reflective thought process.[2]

MARY, DID YOU KNOW?

Finally, according to Bill Mounce's Greek Dictionary, *symballō* means "to dispute with; to confer with, meet with; to ponder; to engage in (war); (mid.) to help, assist."³

FOR THOSE OF US, SUCH AS MYSELF, that are not theologians or scholars, let's break it down just a little more. Mary thoughtfully considered and reflected upon the events and messages she had experienced, keeping them deeply in her heart. I believe that she had a lot to think about.

Not just the angel that had come to her, but the fact that she actually became pregnant without having had sex. Then she sees her cousin, Elizabeth, and there was an outpouring of Holy Spirit-inspired words through each of them. Then, after she births the child, all these different men arrive and share their own experiences, gifts, and insights concerning this Child that she had brought forth. *How did they even know?* Her heart was full of questions, reflections, thoughts that she kept rolling around in her mind and heart. She had to wonder, *"Just who is this Child that I birthed?"*

Now his parents went to Jerusalem every year at the feast of the Passover. And when he was twelve years old, they went up to Jerusalem after the custom of the feast. And when they had fulfilled the days, as they returned, the child Jesus tarried behind in Jerusalem; and Joseph and his mother knew not *of it*. But they, supposing him to have been in the company, went a day's journey; and they sought him among *their* kinsfolk and acquaintance. And when they found him not, they turned back again to Jerusalem, seeking him.

And it came to pass, that after three days they found him in the temple, sitting in the midst of the doctors, both hearing them, and asking them questions. And all that heard him were astonished at his understanding and answers. And when they saw him, they were amazed: and his mother said unto him,

> Son, why hast thou thus dealt with us? behold, thy father and I have sought thee sorrowing.

MARY, DID YOU KNOW?

And he said unto them,

> **HOW IS IT THAT YE SOUGHT ME? WIST YE NOT THAT I MUST BE ABOUT MY FATHER'S BUSINESS?**

And they understood not the saying which he spake unto them. And he went down with them, and came to Nazareth, and was subject unto them: but his mother kept all these sayings in her heart.

And Jesus increased in wisdom and stature, and in favour with God and man.[4]

....but his mother kept all these sayings in her heart.

Let's look at this word, "kept" from the *Theological Dictionary of the New Testament* (TDNT). It is translated *diatēreō* (διατηρέω), which denotes "to keep continually or carefully," emphasizing a sustained and attentive preservation of events or words in one's memory.[5]

In Luke 2:51, the term "kept" translates the Greek verb διατηρέω (diatēreō), which combines the

> preposition "διά" (dia, meaning "through" or "thoroughly") with the verb "τηρέω" (tēreō, meaning "to keep" or "to guard"). This compound verb conveys the sense of thoroughly preserving or carefully maintaining something. In this context, it signifies Mary's diligent and continual reflection on the events and sayings concerning Jesus.[6]

Meaning that Mary was continuously absorbed with remembrances. She carried and held the significant events and words related to her son, Jesus, deeply in her heart.

MARY, THE MOTHER OF JESUS, HAD A lot to think about. From the time of His conception to the days of His crucifixion, resurrection and beyond.

She definitely knew something.

O Tannenbaum

THE CHRISTMAS TREE ACROSS CULTURES AND TIME

Growing up in my mother's house, Christmas Eve was an exciting event. We had three traditions that you might resonate with. After we had each taken our baths, everyone assembled in the living room, gathered around the tree. My brother, sister, and I would get to open one gift each. And what was inside? Pajamas. Every year.

Bath. New pajamas. Then pictures. Did I mention that we all had the jammies all matched? It was a lot of fun. And the neat thing is how these tradition have continued over the years. First as adults, and then as parents, my siblings and I have continued the family pajama trend. Especially my sister, her husband, and my three gorgeous nephews. They made it something of an art form.

Our Christmas trees were big, freshly flocked, decorated with multi-colored ornaments, and the classic color-wheel. Our Christmases were also quite lavish, and underneath the tree were oodles of presents. Mom did Christmas up like a real family party, no one was ever left out. Meaning that if we had guests or some of her other [love adopted] children staying over, they also received a new set of sleepwear. And all the while, we would drink eggnog or hot chocolate (for the children), and munch on snacks until bedtime. There would always be some form of music, softly playing on the stereo. Christmas jazz. Yeah. Good times.

Now that our children have attained adulthood, we've veered into a different direction. More recently it's been electric blankets, or some kind of comfy, cozy type of quilted snuggle contraption. One way or another, our childhood traditions have extended to Mom's grandchildren, and as they settle into parenting, I can see them being carried on with their children. Three generations of actions based upon our own oral traditions. Childhood can sometimes be very cool. 🔔🔔🔔

A Little History About Christmas Trees

The Christmas tree as we know it today evolved from ancient customs and rituals involving evergreen plants. Pagan practices dating back to around 2000 BCE included decorating branches with fruit, nuts, and candles as offerings to deities or symbols of prosperity. These adornments were meant to symbolize eternal life, provide protection, serve as appeasements, and invoke blessings or hope for better days during the winter solstice.

These customs were later adapted by Christians, particularly in 16th-century Germany, where the Christmas tree became a symbol of Christ's birth and eternal life. In medieval Europe, trees were adorned with candles, which represented stars in the heavens, an idea attributed to Martin Luther. Over time, decorations shifted to include glass ornaments with Christian symbols like stars and angels, then nativity scenes, blended the sacred with cultural traditions.

By the 19th century, Christmas trees had become a central symbol in holiday celebrations across Europe and America. Incidentally, we can also thank the Germans for our tinsel, orbs, baubles, and other types of glass ornaments. Hans Greiner, a descendant of the founder of Lauscha's first glassworks, began producing glass ornaments shaped like fruits and nuts using hand-blown techniques combined with molds in 1847. And that is when the tradition of adorning Christmas trees with glass orbs—ornaments known as *Glaskugeln*—commonly known as baubles, originated. In mid-19th century Germany.[1]

So, how did ornaments get to America and become a standard part of our Christmas holiday decor? By the late 19th century, glass baubles grew in popularity as they were exported across Europe. In the 1880s they were discovered by Mr. F.W. Woolworth, and he began to import them to the United States, where they became a major retail success. By 1890, Woolworth's stores were selling $25 million worth of these ornaments. During the late 1930s, Mr. Woolworth collaborated with the Corning Company to make ornaments more affordable for everyone. They created these mass-produced glass ornaments using machinery initially designed for light bulb production—and that's what led to the creation of the "Shiny Brite" brand ornaments.[2]

THE TRADITIONS SURROUNDING Christmas trees have sparked debates over their pagan oral traditions, so it should not be a surprise that Christmas tree traditions can be categorized into two primary influences: Pagan and Sacred. To some, Christmas trees are just part of the holiday fun. Whereas other Christians view the practice of decorating trees as distasteful or even sinful, citing scriptures like Jeremiah 10:1-5.

> You people of Israel, listen to what the LORD has to say to you. The LORD says, "Do not start following pagan religious practices. Do not be in awe of signs that occur in the sky even though the nations hold them in awe. For the religion of these people

is worthless. They cut down a tree in the forest, and a craftsman makes it into an idol with his tools. He decorates it with overlays of silver and gold. He uses hammer and nails to fasten it together so that it will not fall over."[3]

Some argue that this passage of scripture condemns decorating holiday trees, though scholars generally agree that the prophet's message refers to the crafting of wooden idols covered in silver and gold, idols created for worship, not holiday decorations. In contrast, others embrace the tree as a festive element of Christmas, emphasizing its symbolic connection to eternal life and Christ as the "Light of the World."

Historical evidence suggests that while the tree's origins may be rooted in pagan customs, Christians adapted the practice to align with their theology. Still, some will continue to point to these paganistic origins of Christmas and stand firm in their boycott.

If you do a little research, you will learn about the broader context of his words, released to condemn Israel's choice of idolatry over God.

Seriously, the intent of this passage is not about the symbolic use of natural elements in celebrations. Read a bit further and you can see that the conversation had nothing to do with how you decorate your home in December. The prophet's concern was not a holiday tree covered in silver and gold tinsel.[4]

> I said, "There is no one like you, LORD. You are great. And you are renowned for your power. Everyone should revere you, O King of all nations, because you deserve to be revered. For there is no one like you among any of the wise people of the nations nor among any of their kings. The people of those nations are both stupid and foolish. Instruction from a wooden idol is worthless! Hammered-out silver is brought from Tarshish and gold is brought from Ufaz to cover those idols. They are the handiwork of carpenters and goldsmiths. They are clothed in blue and purple clothes. They are all made by skillful workers. The LORD is the only true God. He is the living God and the everlasting King. When he shows his anger the

earth shakes. None of the nations can stand up to his fury. You people of Israel should tell those nations this: 'These gods did not make heaven and earth. They will disappear from the earth and from under the heavens.' The LORD is the one who by his power made the earth. He is the one who by his wisdom established the world. And by his understanding he spread out the skies.[5]

TYPICALLY, THE TYPE OF TREE FOUND IN different homes during the Christmas holiday season depends upon that great real estate term: Location. Location. Location. That's because different trees grow in different regions. However, for those into the symbolic meaning of each type of tree, the choice of fir, evergreen, spruce, and other tree types is intentional.

That's because, according to knowledge obtained by oral tradition, the Fir, Evergreen,

Spruce, Pine, and Cedar branches each have deep symbolic meanings that have evolved over centuries, blending that which is sacred with that which is cultural. A brief compare/contrast for each type of greenery gives us a little insight into the reasons they meant so much to the people of the times.

Evergreens, Fir, Spruce, Pine, and Cedar trees each have a symbolic meaning to the people of old. While the evergreen symbolized eternal life and hope, even in the cold of winter—nation's triumph over death, the fir tree was seen as a representation of righteousness, light, and purity. These are the trees that were adorned with candles during medieval times, ostensibly in Christian imagery to represent the light of the world.

Spruce trees symbolized strength and protection, they were thought to have the power to ward off evil spirits, something of great importance to the winter solstice festivities. The pine trees are attributed to be symbols of life (vitality) and endurance, and then there is the cedar tree.

In the Bible, we read about the growth of cedars of Lebanon (Psalm 92:12), and that's what cedar trees symbolize: growth, strength, and spiritual rootedness. There is a lot of interesting reading to be done regarding the history of Christmas trees, and both the pagan and Christian festival properties. [6]

Christmas Trees Across Cultures

It's interesting to realize how far-reaching the influence of the kingdoms of this world has spread. Centuries before and since the birth of Christ, the influence in various cultures has had a common tone.

Across cultures and time, from Germany to Japan, the Christmas tree has been celebrated in various forms. For some, it represents Christian faith; for others, it is a secular holiday symbol. The rich history of the Christmas tree highlights its enduring cultural significance. The history is rich indeed. [7]

THE SONG IS STILL KNOWN AS BOTH "*O Christmas Tree*" and "*O Tannenbaum,*" which is the original German title. The English translation, "*O Christmas Tree*" is an adaptation. Tannenbaum, the German word for "fir tree," is not historically tied to Christmas. The early versions of the song, inspired by oral German folk traditions, with early versions appearing as far back as the 16th century, celebrated the fir tree for its evergreen nature, which to them was a symbol of faithfulness and constancy.

What is known as the modern version is attributed to Ernst Anschütz in 1824. The story told of the tree's enduring qualities. The symbolism that reflected Christmas was mixed in around the 19th century, which is about the time that the Christmas tree became a central symbol of holiday celebrations, and when *O Tannenbaum*" was adapted into a carol associated with the season. And by the way, the German lyrics are quite different from the English ones. Both versions share the same melody, but the cultural context and lyrical focus differ. While *O Tannenbaum* focuses on the steadfast, unchanging green foliage of the fir tree, *O Christmas Tree* celebrates the tree as part of the Christmas tradition.[8]

· · ·

My intention in writing this book is not to persuade anyone about how to celebrate Christmas. To tree or not to tree is not the question. This dialogue merely provides snapshots of various holiday celebrations through the ages, exploring the embrace and rejection of the King and kingdom given to us. Amen.

Not A Creature Was Stirring

THE STORY OF ST. NICHOLAS

Through the ages, we have witnessed various attempts to replace God's message to His creation with pagan or secular rituals, and Christian efforts to replace celebrations and festivals with the message of God's true light. Why not just create something new?

Let's define *paganism* for the sake of these discussions. The word *paganism* derives from classical Latin word, *pāgānus*, meaning *rural*, or *rustic*, and later, *civilian*. The term pagan was not meant to be complementary, in fact, the notion itself is attributed to originate from the early Christian Church, around the fourth century. It was the antithesis to the process of Christian self-definition. In fact, throughout history it was generally used in a derogatory manner. The reference was then directed toward people in the Roman Empire who practiced polytheism or some other religion that did not embrace Judaism. Paganism was considered to be the religion of peasants, the rural or rustic people. Oh, and there were other terms used as well, *hellene, gentile,* and *heathen* to name a few. [1]

During Christmas time, there are a lot of references to the mythical Santa Claus, which somehow became interspersed with the real person known as St. Nicholas, a 3rd or 4th century Greek bishop famous for his charitable acts, often carried out anonymously. Although we won't do an exhaustive introduction to him here, St. Nicholas is an interesting character to study.

He is considered to be the patron saint of children, sailors, and merchants, and was celebrated with his own December 6th feast day—a day marked in many cultures, particularly in Europe, by acts of kindness *and* the giving of gifts. This date was also the time of the Roman celebration of Saturnalia, when gifts were exchanged to honor Saturn, the god of agriculture—and the reason Christmas as we know it was originally frowned upon the New England part of the colonies.

By way of oral traditions, tales were shared about his miraculous acts, compassion and protection—all of which has made him a beloved figure in both religious and secular traditions.[2]

It was the Dutch settlers of the 17th century that brought the tradition of Sinterklaas to America, particularly in New York, then known as New Amsterdam. This Dutch version of Saint Nicholas was the primary influence in shaping the American Santa Claus. As for the flying sleigh and some of the other folklore, we can thank Washington Irving, who wrote *A History of New York*, using the pscudonym Diedrich Knickerbocker, in which he writes of a dream in which St. Nicholas soars over treetops in a flying wagon—a kind of prelude towards a more magical, red-suited mythical person[3].

DURING MY SCHOOL YEARS, I participated in a number of choral groups and choirs. To this day my internal jukebox can pull forth songs that fall under the *Trivial Pursuit* or *Name That Tune* categories. One popular song we would sing was based on the poem written by Clement Clarke Moore. Even as I write this, the melody line for this particular poem is running through my mind. It's also fun to read aloud, something that has been done by more than one celebrity.[4]

And so, I present to you, *A Visit From St. Nicholas*.

A Visit from St. Nicholas
Clement Clarke Moore

'Twas the night before Christmas, when all through the house. Not a creature was stirring, not even a mouse;
The stockings were hung by the chimney with care,
In hopes that St. Nicholas soon would be there;
The children were nestled all snug in their beds;
While visions of sugar-plums

danced in their heads;
And mamma in her 'kerchief, and I in my cap,
Had just settled our brains for a long winter's nap,
When out on the lawn there arose such a clatter,
I sprang from my bed to see what was the matter.
Away to the window I flew like a flash,
Tore open the shutters and threw up the sash.
The moon on the breast of the new-fallen snow,
Gave a lustre of midday to objects below,
When what to my wondering eyes did appear,
But a miniature sleigh and eight tiny rein-deer,
With a little old driver so lively and quick,
I knew in a moment he must be St. Nick.
More rapid than eagles his coursers they came,
And he whistled, and shouted, and called them by name:
"Now, Dasher! now, Dancer! now Prancer and Vixen!
On, Comet! on, Cupid! on, Donder and Blitzen!
To the top of the porch! to the top of the wall!
Now dash away! dash away! dash away all!"
As leaves that before the wild hurricane fly,
When they meet with an obstacle, mount to the sky;
So up to the housetop the coursers they flew
With the sleigh full of toys, and St. Nicholas too—

NOT A CREATURE WAS STIRRING

And then, in a twinkling, I heard on the roof
The prancing and pawing of each little hoof.
As I drew in my head, and was turning around,
Down the chimney St. Nicholas came with a bound.
He was dressed all in fur, from his head to his foot,
And his clothes were all tarnished with ashes and soot;
A bundle of toys he had flung on his back,
And he looked like a pedler just opening his pack.
His eyes—how they twinkled! his dimples, how merry!
His cheeks were like roses, his nose like a cherry!
His droll little mouth was drawn up like a bow,
And the beard on his chin was as white as the snow;
The stump of a pipe he held tight in his teeth,
And the smoke, it encircled his head like a wreath;
He had a broad face and a little round belly
That shook when he laughed, like a bowl full of jelly.
He was chubby and plump, a right jolly old elf,
And I laughed when I saw him, in spite of myself;
A wink of his eye and a twist of his head
Soon gave me to know I had nothing to dread;

He spoke not a word, but went straight to his work,
And filled all the stockings; then turned with a jerk,
And laying his finger aside of his nose,
And giving a nod, up the chimney he rose;
He sprang to his sleigh, to his team gave a whistle,
And away they all flew like the down of a thistle.
But I heard him exclaim, ere he drove out of sight—
"Happy Christmas to all, and to all a good night!"[5]

Hark! Hear The Bells

THE STORIES THEY TELL

Once upon a prayer time, I had a conversation with the Holy Spirit regarding different aspects of praise, worship, and intercessory prayer. Now this took place before I began to study music from a true Kingdom of Heaven perspective. When He began to nudge me in the direction of sounds, frequencies, and being intentional in the spirit realm, I was granted a glimpse of all things beautiful in the praise-prayer arena.

What did I see?

I saw how God's words spoken through us in intercession take on the form of various instruments and weapons, all designed to enforce the defeat of the works of the devil. I even caught a glimpse of how God's spoken words form into walls, hands, or whatever is necessary to dismantle weapons or hindrances formed against us. It happens as His word is released into the earthly atmosphere through our mouths.

In quantum faith terminology, that means I actually began to see the how-to of what Jesus means in Mark 11, when He tells us to use God's faith to vanquish and conquer the so-called impossible. We do so by releasing His Kingdom possibilities into this earth realm. I caught a glimpse of how we are to move forward to take and occupy our assigned territory. It is accomplished by wielding the royal power we have access to through His Kingdom.

It turns out that a number of the struggles and setbacks I've encountered in my own life stem from a lack of consistency in my words and actions. The Holy Spirit then let me know that I was below par in the way that I lived my life, and it was time to step up to His Kingdom standard, which I have begun to do. And oh what fun it is. Alas, that message and those lessons are for another time, in a different book. We're talking about Christmas through the ages, so here's what I want to share.

Although I do not recall the first time that I heard *Carol of the Bells*, the song resonates with me for several reasons, in part because of this God encounter I just referred to. You see, what I was privileged to glimpse and learn in that encounter is what kind of weaponry my own voice becomes in that realm. He made it very clear to me that when He works through me as an instrument of His righteousness, I become a bell that He sounds. How cool is that! This may explain why I have listened to *Carol of the Bells* on continuous play for these past 10 years or so.

What I was privileged to see is that this transformation primarily happens in times of honest praise and worship—not from participating in a bouncy song service—but the things that happen when it is just the two of us. Intimacy reveals different elements in worship and prayer times. The closest comparison I can use to illustrate what I mean is the intimacy that takes place between lovers. There is an inner sanctum rawness that allows you to say things to Him that you won't or can't say in front of others. And that's when resonance occurs. So, let's talk about Christmas bells, songs, and the power of words fitly chosen.

The Sound of Bells

Bells have long been more than instruments of sound—they are carriers of messages, symbols of joy, and echoes of celebration. From the grand peal of church bells announcing the birth of Christ to the cheerful ringing of handbells in carols and those holiday donation stations, bell sounds bring the meaning of the season to life.

Each note resonates with a timeless truth: *Light has come into the world.* There are two really beautiful carols that resonate with the sound of bells.

One began as a poem, the other a folksong.

I Heard the Bells on Christmas Day

It was the year 1863, during the tumult of the American Civil War, when Henry Wadsworth Longfellow penned the words to a poem that depicted the pain and despair of his life. It was the heart cry of a man wrestling with deep personal grief and national sorrow. That poem would later become the carol known as, *I Heard the Bells on Christmas Day.*

It had only been two years since Mr. Longfellow had experienced several personal tragedies: his wife Fannie died a tragic death by fire, Henry sustained both physical and emotional permanent scars in his attempt to save her. Later, his son Charles enlisted in the Union Army without his father's blessing, then was severely injured in battle. Thankfully, he was able to return home.

It's an interesting thing about bells. In times of joy, they peal and resound. But when tragedy is in our midst, we say that the bells are tolling. Such was the case described by Mr. Longfellow. The Christmas bells were tolling about "peace on earth, goodwill to men." Meaning he wasn't feeling any of that, instead the bells seemed to be mocking the current reality of his life and the Civil wartime injustice of the world around him. What was there to be cheery about on that Christmas morning? His family had been fragmented, and his nation divided. Yet it was the sound of church bells ringing through the air on that December morning in 1863, that stirred him to action.

BUT THE MERCY OF GOD PULLED HIM into a dialogue, and on paper Mr. Longfellow confronted the tension and pain of his world in response to the proclamation of the bells. He spoke to many hearts, his words weighing the power of despair and the power of faith in the unyielding, unfailing promises of God, despite the tangible and visible brokenness of the world. It may sound dramatic in the telling, and it should. Because it is what he wrote that reminds us that all too often, darkness attempts to steal our hopes and dreams.

> "And in despair, I bowed my head;
> 'There is no peace on earth,' I said,
> 'For hate is strong,
> And mocks the song
> Of peace on earth, good-will to men.'"

But Longfellow's journey through grief did not end there. As he reflected, his ears attuned once more to the persistent ringing of the bells. Their message grew louder, deeper, and truer, as if defying the despair around him. The bells seemed to proclaim a reality beyond the visible, a reminder that God's presence and righteousness endure through every trial.

"Then pealed the bells more loud and deep:
'God is not dead, nor doth He sleep;
The Wrong shall fail,
The Right prevail,
With peace on earth, good-will to men.'"

The poem that he wrote that day was published two years later in the December issue of a short-lived literary magazine, *The Continental Monthly (1862-1864)*, under the title *Christmas Bells*. It was now the year 1865, and other people had the opportunity to witness Henry Wadsworth Longfellow's personal and national grief in the time of the Civil War. Perhaps they saw hope for themselves through his words. It became first a hymn, then a carol when English organist John Baptiste Calkin first set the words to a melody known as *Waltham*, in 1872.

The popularized version became a well-loved carol in 1956, when Johnny Marks, best known for *Rudolph the Red-Nosed Reindeer*, composed another version and brought *I Saw The Bells On Christmas Day* to new generations.[1]

While *I Heard the Bells on Christmas Day* resonates with a message of hope in God, *Carol of the Bells* vibrates at a different frequency altogether, calling us to consider the melodiously joyful ring of harmony, rhythm, and celebration. Whereas Longfellow's carol draws us into an introspective resolve to trust God and persevere in the face of adversity, *Carol of the Bells*, this carol with roots in a Ukrainian folksong sweeps us into the dance.

The History of "Carol of the Bells"

The song we now know as *Carol of the Bells* originated as a Ukrainian folk chant called *Shchedryk*, composed by Mykola Leontovych in 1916. This four-note melody, inspired by ancient Slavic chants, was part of the New Year's tradition of *shchedrivky*, which celebrated prosperity and the coming of spring.

There is a lot of political history behind the formation of the choirs that performed this song as they traveled to different parts of the globe. But it was in 1921 that the Ukrainian National Chorus introduced *Shchedryk* to sold-out audiences at Carnegie Hall. It was love at first listen, a truth I can totally relate to. Then, in 1936, Peter J. Wilhousky, an American of Ukrainian descent, adapted the melody into English, transforming it into *Carol of the Bells*. His lyrics gave the song new life as a Christmas carol, with bells symbolizing the joyful tidings of Christ's birth.

I'm not alone in regarding this carol as one with timeless appeal—it has an amazing ability to convey the joy and wonder of the season, inspires movement, and bridge cultures and traditions through its universal message. In my opinion, this carol is also a really cool swaying dance song – it just inspires movement, even for those of us that don't know how to dance. The song's timeless appeal lies in its ability to convey the joy and wonder of the season, bridging cultures and traditions through its universal message.[2]

. . .

History, Symbolism, Science, and Frequencies

The two bell carols we've looked at stimulate our souls in different manners. What is at work here is what some refer to as emotional frequencies, said to align with the human voice. According to some of the scientific sources and speculative studies, this is because the frequencies of bells resonate with the call and response pattern that will call for, or re-call our emotional responses. That's what music does. Just think about which songs get you going, which ones make you sad, the songs you're quick to shut off, and the ones that call you to crank it up and respond as soon as you hear the first note.

This is intentional, and that's what well-played bell, string, wind, and percussion sounds do. Now, it doesn't take long to connect the dots and realize that the same musical frequencies that call our spirit or emotions to respond have the same effect in the spiritual realm.

Bells used for sacred ceremony and celebration will vibrate at frequencies that symbolize clarity, purity, and worship. Likewise, bells used for paganistic rituals during solstice celebrations vibrated at frequencies to dispel darkness and ward off evil spirits. It was another form of worship.

This is a study that requires more room for discussion than we have here. But I want to make one last point as we've primarily been discussing Christmas carols—some of which we know have origins in pagan rituals. Bells were and are crafted and tuned for specific effect. The overtones and harmonics created sounds that are meant to linger in the air. So here are the last few facts about bell song frequencies, vibrations, and waves.

Bell Frequencies

Bells frequencies vary at a wide range dependent upon size, shape, and material. These are the factors that influence the vibrations and frequencies produced when a bell is struck, resulting in its characteristic resonance.

1. Fundamental Frequency: The lowest and strongest tone, perceived as the primary pitch.

2. Overtones (Harmonics): Higher frequencies

that enrich the bell's sound and create its tonal complexity.

3. Hum Tone: A subtle low-frequency vibration that underpins the overall sound.

4. Strike Tone: The immediate pitch heard when the clapper strikes the bell.

Well-cast, tuned bell materials vary in combinations of bronze, copper and tin mixtures, steel, silver, brass. And yes there are crystal bells, too. Their shapes are large and thick (lower frequency, slower vibration), small and thin (higher frequency, faster vibration). Those done well can harmonize with their overtones (lovely sound), while the inferior cast bells produce dissonant tones.

Putting It All Together

When struck, a bell vibrates in complex patterns, producing sound waves that propagate through the air. How does it happen?

First the bell's shape amplifies certain frequencies, creating a ringing sound that carries over long distances. This is Resonance. Every strike of the bell Waveforms: Each strike creates longitudinal and transverse waves, interacting to form the bell's distinctive tonal character. These are the Waveforms. And finally, the amount of time the sound sustains is determined by the material and size of the bell. And this is when those large bronze bells shine, sustaining their several seconds. This is known as Decay Time.[3]

But remember, sound lingers in the atmosphere, and it should also emanate from within you and me. Like the continual message of *I Heard The Bells on Christmas Day* and the joyous thrill of *Carol of the Bells*, we are called to be God's instruments in the earth, resounding with His truth, hope, and love, royal offspring shining the light of our Father's kingdom to dispel the darkness of this world.

I Have A Little Dreidel

A BRIEF LOOK AT HANUKKAH

Because it is a celebration that takes place during the traditional Christmas holiday season, let's say just a few words about Hanukkah (also spelled Chanukah).

First and foremost, let's establish the fact that Hanukkah, the Festival of Lights is **not** a Jewish substitute for Christmas. The celebration of the Festival of Lights precedes the birth of Jesus by hundreds of years. The stories pertaining to Jesus and Hanukkah can be found in John 10, verse 22.

"Then came the Festival of Dedication at Jerusalem. It was winter, and Jesus was in the temple courts walking in Solomon's Colonnade."

Let's look at this same verse in *The Scriptures 2009* version:

> *"At that time the Ḥanukkah came to be in Yerushalayim, and it was winter. Footnote: Feast of Dedication, during which candles are lit every evening to commemorate Maccabean victory over Greeks in 165 BCE."* (John 10:22, The Scriptures ISR)

It was during this festival that Jesus proclaimed His unity with the Father, *"I and my Father are one."* Then, by declaring, *"I am the Light of the World,"* * He not only linked Himself to the light celebrated during Hanukkah, He established His sonship identity and authority, as He aligned Himself with the eternal power of the Kingdom of God.

LET'S REVISIT OUR UNDERSTANDING OF oral traditions and written records for a moment. The legacy found within Jewish festivals like Hanukkah are rooted in strong oral components, with rituals, songs, and

---

* John 10:30, John 8:12 respectively.

storytelling that continues to be passed down through generations. It is through Jewish oral tradition that the story of Hanukkah was told, alongside other teachings and narratives, preserving this account until the written texts were established.

Hanukkah commemorates the rededication of the Second Temple following the Maccabees' victory over the Seleucid Greeks. The menorah in the rededicated Temple burned miraculously for eight days during the Maccabean revolt, even though there was only enough consecrated oil to last for one day. This event is central to the celebration of Hanukkah, symbolizing divine intervention and faith's perseverance.

The story of this miracle is preserved through Jewish oral traditions, later codified in the Talmud. This text formalized the account within the Jewish canon and connected the story to broader religious teachings. Tractate Shabbat 21b provides the most famous written record of the Hanukkah miracle, emphasizing God's divine providence and light overcoming darkness, themes that resonate deeply with the celebration.[1]

In case you're wondering, the Talmud, a central text of Rabbinic Judaism, is a vast collection of Jewish teachings and interpretations. It consists of two primary parts:

1. Mishnah (c. 200 CE): The written collection of Jewish oral laws and traditions. It outlines the foundational legal principles and practices of Judaism.
2. Gemara (c. 500 CE): A commentary and discussion that expands on the laws of the Mishnah, exploring theological and ethical questions, and incorporating narratives, parables, and debates.

Because the Talmud serves as a guide for Jewish law (Halakha), ethics, customs, and theology, it is not a single book but a vast collection of discussions that represent centuries of rabbinic thought and interpretation.

You can find more resources regarding the two parts and two versions of the Talmud

(Babylonian and Jerusalem) in our reference section.²

Historical and Cultural Roots of Hanukkah

To fully understand Hanukkah, we need to step back and look at its historical context, which begins with Alexander the Great. When Alexander's empire was divided after his death in 323 BCE, his generals inherited control of different regions. Judea eventually fell under the rule of the Seleucid Empire, founded by Seleucus I Nicator.

By the time of Antiochus IV Epiphanes, the Seleucid rulers had adopted policies aimed at spreading the Hellenistic culture. Antiochus IV, however, took this to an extreme, making it a requirement for life. He desecrated the Temple in Jerusalem, outlawed Jewish religious practices, and forced sacrifices to Greek gods. His decrees, including the prohibition of Sabbath observance and Torah study, were intended to obliterate Jewish identity.

Antiochus IV's regime suppressed Jewish religious practices through vile actions, desecrating the Temple in Jerusalem and forcing the people to adopt Hellenistic customs on threat of death. His decrees included the outlawing of key Jewish practices such as Sabbath observance, circumcision, and Torah study. The Temple was defiled when a pagan altar was erected for sacrifices to Zeus were performed. These acts of desecration deeply offended some of the Jewish people, strengthening their resolve to resist.

But the truth is, not everyone resisted. There were some that preferred to embrace the Hellenistic cultural expression because they liked it. Others did not willingly embrace the renouncement of their faith, they just did not have the courage to stand. The fear of man is a snare we do not want to fall into.*

It's the same in today's society—some in the Christian faith buy into the mindsets and ways of the secular kingdoms of this world, thinking and acting in conformity to societal pressure. Truly, the only way we can effectively stand is by putting our trust in God alone. The culture of the Kingdom of God requires that we stand

---

* The fear of man brings a snare, but one who trusts in the Lord will be protected. Proverbs 29:25 NASB.

firm against compromise, even when it's not popular or convenient. Maybe there are areas in your own life where you're tempted to compromise on the will of the King. Now is a great time to reflect and change your thinking and your actions (repent). Our true source of spiritual strength and power is courtesy of the Kingdom of God.

The books of 1 Maccabees and 2 Maccabees, which are part of the Apocrypha, provide the account of the Seleucid Empire and the reign of Antiochus IV Epiphanes. This is the history and details of the actions that lead to the Maccabean Revolt. This includes the oppressive and evil decrees of Antiochus IV and the resistance of the Jewish people.

Stories like *Chanah and her Seven Sons*, found in 2 and 4 Maccabees, illustrate the courage and faith that defined this resistance. When faced with the choice of breaking Jewish dietary laws or facing death, one by one, Chanah's sons chose death over compromise. One by one, they were tortured and killed, yet they refused to betray their God. Chanah's unwavering faith as she watched her beloved children die is heartrending. Yet, she encouraged her sons to remain steadfast, and in the process has inspired countless others to hold firm in their beliefs.

SIMILARLY, ELEAZAR THE SCRIBE, AN elderly Torah scholar, chose death rather than compromise his faith. His public refusal to eat forbidden food served as a powerful act of defiance, demonstrating that faithfulness to God outweighed even the threat of death. The account of Eleazar the Scribe is found in the Apocrypha, specifically in 2 Maccabees 6:18–31. This passage narrates Eleazar's refusal to eat pork, as mandated by the Seleucid authorities, and his subsequent martyrdom for adhering to Jewish law. [3]

THESE HEARTBREAKING, TRAGIC ACTS of resistance were not in vain. They ignited a collective determination among the Jewish people to fight back. Judah Maccabee, a key leader of the revolt, led strategic military campaigns that defied the odds, defeating the much larger Seleucid forces. The revolt culminated in the recapture and rededication of the Second Temple in 165 BCE, and still resounds the triumph of the resilient, steadfast and immoveable human spirit that refuses to fold in the face of adversity.

You can find this information online on sites such as BibleGateway.com. The links for these stories are provided in the reference section of this book.[4]

Hanukkah Traditions for Children

Being that Hanukkah is a celebration of triumph, there is a joyous side. Let's take a quick look at some of the fun traditions of this season. The enduring legacy is carried forward through its traditions. One of the ways we learn is as we play, and many of the lessons designed to engage children and teach them the history and values of the holiday and their heritage are handed down through stories and games. This causes me to wonder, did a young Jesus of Nazareth also sing these or similar songs and play these types of games?

. . .

THE DREIDEL GAME IS ONE OF THE most beloved Hanukkah customs. The dreidel, a four-sided spinning top, features Hebrew letters—Nun (נ), Gimel (ג), Hei (ה), and Shin (ש)—representing the phrase, *Nes Gadol Haya Sham* ("A great miracle happened there").

Each player starts with an equal number of game pieces, such as chocolate coins (gelt), nuts, or candies. Players take turns spinning the dreidel, and the letter (Nun (נ), Gimel (ג), Hei (ה), and Shin (ש) that lands face up determines the outcome. They do nothing, take everything in the pot, take half of the pot, or add one piece to pot. They continue to spin the dreidel until one player has successfully collected all of the pieces.

Children's Hanukkah Storybooks

Music and storytelling play a central role in Hanukkah celebrations. Songs like, *I Have a Little Dreidel* and *Hanukkah, Oh Hanukkah* are sung in great fun. As you can guess, the atmosphere is joyous. Children are taught the stories of the Maccabees as a part of their own legacy, the miracle of the oil and the menorah, and tales of bravery and commitment like that of Chanah and her seven sons. In so doing, they are taught applicable principles for life and living.

Books are a wonderful way to introduce children to Hanukkah's rich traditions. Especially when they are read aloud. Visit a site such as Chabad.org/kids to find age appropriate titles online. There are a few that also animated. Eric Kimmel's *Hershel and the Hanukkah Goblins* is available in online book stores, and is also on YouTube (the link is in the **References & Resources** at the end of this book). Other books to look into include:

- Ellen Fischer's *Latke, the Lucky Dog*
- David A. Adler's *The Story of Hanukkah*
- Eric Kimmel's *Hanukkah Bear*

- Tanya and Richard Simon's *Oskar and the Eight Blessings*

There are a vast number of resources for the games, songs, videos, and stories of Hanukkah for children. A few are listed for you in the reference section.[5]

Festivals, Feasts and The Kingdom Message of Jesus

As you study the messages preached by Jesus of Nazareth, you realize that first and foremost He taught and demonstrated the reality of the power of God and His Kingdom. Woven into the tapestry of both Hanukkah and the Feast of Tabernacles (Sukkot) is the Kingdom message. Jesus was revealed as the Light of the World, His dedication to fulfilling the prophetic will of His Father being the key to His passion.

The Feast of Tabernacles (Sukkot)

The Feast of Tabernacles, or Sukkot, is also mentioned in the Gospels (John 7:1–52). It celebrates God's provision during the Israelites' wilderness journey and anticipates the

Messianic Kingdom. Sukkot is marked by joy, living in a temporary shelter (*sukkah*), and performing rituals involving water and light.

Prophetic people celebrate birth at conception, which is why some trustworthy scholars say, according to the timeline laid out in scripture, that Jesus' birth coincided with Sukkot, symbolizing God "tabernacling" among His people—*the Word became flesh and dwelt among us.* Jesus' proclamation during the festival, *Let anyone who is thirsty come to me and drink,* connects Him to the water-pouring ritual of Sukkot. His life was the poured out offering, making Him our true source of spiritual provision and nourishment.*,6

Sukkot's focus on God's provision and Messianic hope aligns with Jesus' ministry, highlighting Him as the fulfillment of Old Testament prophecies.

Through these festivals and feasts, we can learn how Jesus was connected with the cultural and prophetic symbols familiar to His audience, yet He remained true to one Source, the Kingdom of God. Set on His course, knowledge of and

---

* John 1:14, John 7:37–39

living according to His identity enabled Him to fulfill every aspect of His assigned mission.

As you can see, there are so many rich insights into the resilience of faith, the power of light over darkness, and the importance of dedication—all of which can be attributed to the reality of our Creator King. We are also sent to shine as beacons of light in our daily lives, even in the way we grow to express uncommon joy in the holidays of our time.

Although Hanukkah is not about Christmas, it is about the power of influence that flows from us by our decisions to stand firm and strong in the things of the Kingdom of God. Through the oral traditions of storytelling and song, the history of Hanukkah is an inspiration, able to influence all cultures to seek after God alone and serve Him. As we do, we will also inspire future generations by living out our own stories highlighting the miracles of God and the courage of His people.

You see, at the end of the day, our true reason for celebrating any significant occasion (such as life itself) is always going to be our King. Celebrate your life and the lives of others, and remember to let His light within you outshine the darkness around others.

Chag Urim Sameach ve-Hanukkah Sameach!

Troll The Ancient Yuletide Carol

YULE LOGS AND MISTLETOE

A number of carols refer to yule logs or the yuletide, but the word itself has no origins in Christmas. Instead, *Yuletide* historically was a holiday celebrated by the Germanic peoples. The word itself derives from the Old English word, *geol* or *giuli*, which referred to a paganistic type of midwinter festival.

This term is connected to the Norse *jól*, a pagan celebration around the winter solstice that honored fertility and the rebirth of the sun, and celebrated natural cycles, marking the shortest day and the anticipation of longer daylight.

The suffix, *"tide"* is also from Old English. *tīd*,

meaning "time" or "season," thus we have *Jól-tīd* (*Yuletide*) "the time of Yule."

Although it's not funny, it is interesting to realize that this is another celebration of pagan origin that was whitewashed, or repurposed for Christians. With the Christian influence coming among the Germanic peoples, early Christian missionaries looked for ways to convert them. Instead of taking away their cultural practices and beliefs, they moved to overlay the Yule traditions with Christian theology to honor the Incarnation—the coming of the Light (Christ) into the darkness of the world.

It took a moment or two, but ultimately they succeeded sometime around the 15th century to mix Yule and Christmas together. And the old Norse holiday traditions such as a Yule log, Yule goat and boar, the feasting and singing all became a part of the Christmas celebration.

Thus, *Yule* became synonymous with Christmastide, a celebration of the birth of Jesus Christ.[1]

Now, while the theological intent behind the adoption of Yuletide was meant to reflect the idea of Jesus as the "Sun of Righteousness"

(Malachi 4:2), shining into the spiritual winter of humanity's fallen state, the mixture is still present today, including the use of holly and mistletoe.

The Blending of Yuletide and Christmas

The strongest organized missionary efforts of Christianization of the Germanic peoples occurred between the 6th and 9th centuries, with the people largely converted to Christianity by the 8th and 9th centuries. And that's when the mixture of existing pagan traditions began. The Winter solstice festivals were re-framed, becoming celebrations of Christmas. The holly, mistletoe, and evergreen trees were infused with Christian meanings to appease the people.

Holly *became* a symbol of Jesus' crucifixion—the sharp leaves represented the crown of thorns and the red berries symbolized His blood. However, the original druid practice for holly was to use its perceived protective properties to ward off evil spirits. And during the Yule midwinter festival, it was considered sacred by both the Roman and Celtic cultures because it remained vibrantly green during winter—symbolizing life, staying power, and protection—which due to its evergreen nature, was associated with eternal life.[2]

In the 21st century, Yuletide in and of itself is said to be celebrated within neopaganism circles at winter solstice, including forms of Wicca, as an alternative to Christmas, although they still celebrate the rebirth of the sun[3].

So, the idea behind decking the halls with boughs of holly, and trolling [sing joyously, loudly, unrestrained, and mayhap even boisterously] the ancient yuletide carol (fa la la la la…) has another layer. Holly to the pagan:

This is not intended to bring about condemnation to anyone. Rather, it is interesting in the history of celebrations around the world. And remember, even in the midst of the revelry and some of the other activities that are part of the tapestry, the influence of Christ did and continues to touch a number of people.

'Twas The Birthday of A King

THE BEST CHRISTMAS STORY EVER!

In our church, *Astounding Love! A Global Church Fellowship & Training Center*, we have a few traditions of our own. One is our unusual ways to celebrate. When Christmastime comes around, in place of a pageant, play, or cantata, each member or family is invited to sing, read, or tell a story as part of our family gathering. Our celebration style was the catalyst for this book.

On occasion, I've read this compilation of scriptures aloud as my part in our celebration. I decided to gift the reading to all of our members. Well, one thing led to another, and here we are. It is my honor to present, **The Best Christmas Story Ever!**

FORASMUCH AS MANY HAVE TAKEN IN hand to set forth in order a declaration of those things which are most surely believed among us, Even as they delivered them unto us, which from the beginning were eyewitnesses, and ministers of the word; It seemed good to me also, having had perfect understanding of all things from the very first, to write unto thee in order, most excellent Theophilus, That thou mightest know the certainty of those things, wherein thou hast been instructed.

There was in the days of Herod, the king of Judaea, a certain priest named Zacharias, of the course of Abia: and his wife was of the daughters of Aaron, and her name was Elisabeth. And they were both righteous before God, walking in all the commandments and ordinances of the Lord blameless. And they had no child, because that Elisabeth was barren, and they both were now well stricken in years. And it came to pass, that while he executed the priest's office before God in the order of his course, According to the custom of the priest's office, his lot was to burn incense when he went into the temple of the Lord.

And the whole multitude of the people were praying without at the time of incense. And there appeared unto him an angel of the Lord standing on the right side of the altar of incense. And when Zacharias saw him, he was troubled, and fear fell upon him. But the angel said unto him,

> FEAR NOT, ZACHARIAS: FOR THY PRAYER IS HEARD; AND THY WIFE ELISABETH SHALL BEAR THEE A SON, AND THOU SHALT CALL HIS NAME JOHN. AND THOU SHALT HAVE JOY AND GLADNESS; AND MANY SHALL REJOICE AT HIS BIRTH. FOR HE SHALL BE GREAT IN THE SIGHT OF THE LORD, AND SHALL DRINK NEITHER WINE NOR STRONG DRINK; AND HE SHALL BE FILLED WITH THE HOLY GHOST, EVEN FROM HIS MOTHER'S WOMB. AND MANY OF THE CHILDREN OF ISRAEL SHALL HE TURN TO THE LORD THEIR GOD. AND HE SHALL GO BEFORE HIM IN THE SPIRIT AND POWER OF ELIAS, TO TURN THE HEARTS OF THE FATHERS TO THE CHILDREN, AND THE

DISOBEDIENT TO THE WISDOM OF THE JUST; TO MAKE READY A PEOPLE PREPARED FOR THE LORD.

And Zacharias said unto the angel,

> Whereby shall I know this? for I am an old man, and my wife well stricken in years.

And the angel answering said unto him,

> I AM GABRIEL, THAT STAND IN THE PRESENCE OF GOD; AND AM SENT TO SPEAK UNTO THEE, AND TO SHEW THEE THESE GLAD TIDINGS. AND, BEHOLD, THOU SHALT BE DUMB, AND NOT ABLE TO SPEAK, UNTIL THE DAY THAT THESE THINGS SHALL BE PERFORMED, BECAUSE THOU BELIEVEST NOT MY WORDS, WHICH SHALL BE FULFILLED IN THEIR SEASON.

And the people waited for Zacharias, and marvelled that he tarried so long in the temple.

And when he came out, he could not speak unto them: and they perceived that he had seen a vision in the temple: for he beckoned unto them, and remained speechless. And it came to pass, that, as soon as the days of his ministration were accomplished, he departed to his own house. And after those days his wife Elisabeth conceived, and hid herself five months, saying,

> Thus hath the Lord dealt with me in the days wherein he looked on me, to take away my reproach among men.

AND IN THE SIXTH MONTH THE ANGEL Gabriel was sent from God unto a city of Galilee, named Nazareth, To a virgin espoused to a man whose name was Joseph, of the house of David; and the virgin's name was Mary. And the angel came in unto her, and said,

> 66 HAIL, THOU THAT ART HIGHLY FAVOURED, THE LORD IS WITH THEE: BLESSED ART THOU AMONG WOMEN.

And when she saw him, she was troubled at his saying, and cast in her mind what manner of salutation this should be. And the angel said unto her,

> Fear not, Mary: for thou hast found favour with God. And, behold, thou shalt conceive in thy womb, and bring forth a son, and shalt call his name Jesus. He shall be great, and shall be called the Son of the Highest: and the Lord God shall give unto him the throne of his father David: And he shall reign over the house of Jacob for ever; and of his kingdom there shall be no end.

Then said Mary unto the angel,

> How shall this be, seeing I know not a man?

And the angel answered and said unto her,

> THE HOLY GHOST SHALL COME UPON THEE, AND THE POWER OF THE HIGHEST SHALL OVERSHADOW THEE: THEREFORE ALSO THAT HOLY THING WHICH SHALL BE BORN OF THEE SHALL BE CALLED THE SON OF GOD. AND, BEHOLD, THY COUSIN ELISABETH, SHE HATH ALSO CONCEIVED A SON IN HER OLD AGE: AND THIS IS THE SIXTH MONTH WITH HER, WHO WAS CALLED BARREN. FOR WITH GOD NOTHING SHALL BE IMPOSSIBLE.

And Mary said,

> Behold the handmaid of the Lord; be it unto me according to thy word.

And the angel departed from her.

And Mary arose in those days, and went into the hill country with haste, into a city of Juda; And entered into the house of Zacharias, and saluted Elisabeth. And it came to pass, that, when Elisabeth heard the salutation of Mary, the babe leaped in her womb; and Elisabeth was filled with the Holy Ghost: And she spake out with a loud voice, and said,

> Blessed art thou among women, and blessed is the fruit of thy womb. And whence is this to me, that the mother of my Lord should come to me? For, lo, as soon as the voice of thy salutation sounded in mine ears, the babe leaped in my womb for joy. And blessed is she that believed: for there shall be a performance of those things which were told her from the Lord.

And Mary said,

> My soul doth magnify the Lord, And my spirit hath rejoiced in God my Saviour. For he hath regarded the low estate of his handmaiden: for, behold, from henceforth all generations shall call me blessed. For he that is mighty hath done to me great things; and holy is his name. And his mercy is on them that fear him from generation to generation. He hath shewed strength with his arm; he hath scattered the proud in the imagination of their

hearts. He hath put down the mighty from their seats, and exalted them of low degree. He hath filled the hungry with good things; and the rich he hath sent empty away. He hath holpen his servant Israel, in remembrance of his mercy; As he spake to our fathers, to Abraham, and to his seed for ever.

And Mary abode with her about three months, and returned to her own house.

Now Elisabeth's full time came that she should be delivered; and she brought forth a son. And her neighbours and her cousins heard how the Lord had shewed great mercy upon her; and they rejoiced with her. And it came to pass, that on the eighth day they came to circumcise the child; and they called him Zacharias, after the name of his father. And his mother answered and said,

> Not so; but he shall be called John.

And they said unto her,

```
There is none of thy kindred
that is called by this name.
```

And they made signs to his father, how he would have him called. And he asked for a writing table, and wrote, saying, His name is John. And they marvelled all. And his mouth was opened immediately, and his tongue loosed, and he spake, and praised God. And fear came on all that dwelt round about them: and all these sayings were noised abroad throughout all the hill country of Judaea. And all they that heard them laid them up in their hearts, saying,

> What manner of child shall this be! And the hand of the Lord was with him.

And his father Zacharias was filled with the Holy Ghost, and prophesied, saying,

> Blessed be the Lord God of Israel; for he hath visited and redeemed his people, And hath raised up an horn of salvation for us in the house of his servant David; As he spake by the mouth of his holy prophets, which have been since the world

began: That we should be
saved from our enemies, and
from the hand of all that
hate us; To perform the
mercy promised to our
fathers, and to remember his
holy covenant; The oath
which he sware to our father
Abraham, That he would grant
unto us, that we being
delivered out of the hand of
our enemies might serve him
without fear, In holiness
and righteousness before him,
all the days of our life.
And thou, child, shalt be
called the prophet of the
Highest: for thou shalt go
before the face of the Lord
to prepare his ways; To give
knowledge of salvation unto
his people by the remission
of their sins, Through the
tender mercy of our God;
whereby the dayspring from on
high hath visited us, To give
light to them that sit in
darkness and in the shadow of

```
death, to guide our feet into
the way of peace.
```

And the child grew, and waxed strong in spirit, and was in the deserts till the day of his shewing unto Israel.[1]

For God so loved the world, that he gave his only begotten Son, that whosoever believeth in him should not perish, but have everlasting life. For God sent not his Son into the world to condemn the world; but that the world through him might be saved.[2]

Nevertheless the dimness shall not be such as was in her vexation, when at the first he lightly afflicted the land of Zebulun and the land of Naphtali, and afterward did more grievously afflict her by the way of the sea, beyond Jordan, in Galilee of the nations. The people that walked in darkness have seen a great light: they that dwell in the land of the shadow of death, upon them hath the light shined.[3]

For unto us a child is born, unto us a son is given: and the government shall be upon his shoulder: and his name shall be called Wonderful, Counsellor, The mighty God, The everlasting Father, The Prince of Peace. Of the increase of his government and peace there shall be no end, upon the throne of David, and upon his kingdom, to order it, and to establish it with judgment and with justice from henceforth even for ever. The zeal of the LORD of hosts will perform this.[4]

Now the birth of Jesus Christ was on this wise: When as his mother Mary was espoused to Joseph, before they came together, she was found with child of the Holy Ghost. Then Joseph her husband, being a just *man*, and not willing to make her a publick example, was minded to put her away privily. But while he thought on these things, behold, the angel of the Lord appeared unto him in a dream, saying,

> Joseph, thou son of David, fear not to take unto thee Mary thy wife: for that which is conceived in her is of the Holy Ghost. And she

SHALL BRING FORTH A SON, AND THOU SHALT CALL HIS NAME JESUS: FOR HE SHALL SAVE HIS PEOPLE FROM THEIR SINS.

Now all this was done, that it might be fulfilled which was spoken of the Lord by the prophet, saying,

> Behold, a virgin shall be with child, and shall bring forth a son, and they shall call his name Emmanuel, which being interpreted is, God with us.

Then Joseph being raised from sleep did as the angel of the Lord had bidden him, and took unto him his wife: And knew her not till she had brought forth her firstborn son: and he called his name JESUS.[5]

And it came to pass in those days, that there went out a decree from Caesar Augustus, that all the world should be taxed. (And this taxing was first made when Cyrenius was governor of Syria.) And all went to be taxed, every one into his own city. And Joseph also went up from Galilee, out of the city of Nazareth, into Judaea, unto the city of David, which is called

Bethlehem; (because he was of the house and lineage of David:) To be taxed with Mary his espoused wife, being great with child.

And so it was, that, while they were there, the days were accomplished that she should be delivered. And she brought forth her firstborn son, and wrapped him in swaddling clothes, and laid him in a manger; because there was no room for them in the inn.

And there were in the same country shepherds abiding in the field, keeping watch over their flock by night. And, lo, the angel of the Lord came upon them, and the glory of the Lord shone round about them: and they were sore afraid. And the angel said unto them,

> Fear not: for, behold, I bring you good tidings of great joy, which shall be to all people. For unto you is born this day in the city of David a Saviour, which is Christ the Lord. And this shall be a sign unto you; Ye shall find the babe wrapped in swaddling clothes, lying in a manger.

And suddenly there was with the angel a multitude of the heavenly host praising God, and saying,

> Glory to God in the highest, and on earth peace, good will toward men.

And it came to pass, as the angels were gone away from them into heaven, the shepherds said one to another,

'TWAS THE BIRTHDAY OF A KING

Let us now go even unto Bethlehem, and
see this thing which is come to pass,
which the Lord hath made known unto us.

And they came with haste, and found Mary, and Joseph, and the babe lying in a manger. And when they had seen it, they made known abroad the saying which was told them concerning this child. And all they that heard it wondered at those things which were told them by the shepherds. But Mary kept all these things, and pondered them in her heart.

And the shepherds returned, glorifying and praising God for all the things that they had heard and seen, as it was told unto them. And when eight days were accomplished for the circumcising of the child, his name was called JESUS, which was so named of the angel before he was conceived in the womb.

And when the days of her purification according to the law of Moses were accomplished, they brought him to Jerusalem, to present him to the Lord; (As it is written in the law of the Lord, Every male that openeth the womb shall be called holy to the Lord;) And to offer a sacrifice according to that which is said in the law of the Lord, A pair of turtledoves, or two young pigeons.

And, behold, there was a man in Jerusalem, whose name was Simeon; and the same man was just and devout, waiting for the consolation of Israel: and the Holy Ghost was upon him. And it was revealed unto him by the Holy Ghost, that he should not see death, before he had seen the Lord's Christ. And he came by the Spirit into the temple: and when the parents brought in the child Jesus, to do for him after the custom of the law, Then took he him up in his arms, and blessed God, and said,

> Lord, now lettest thou thy servant depart in peace, according to thy word: For mine eyes have seen thy salvation, Which thou hast prepared before the face of all people; A light to lighten the Gentiles, and the glory of thy people Israel.

And Joseph and his mother marvelled at those things which were spoken of him. And Simeon blessed them, and said unto Mary his mother,

> Behold, this child is set for the fall and rising again of many in Israel; and for a

sign which shall be spoken against; (Yea, a sword shall pierce through thy own soul also,) that the thoughts of many hearts may be revealed.

And there was one Anna, a prophetess, the daughter of Phanuel, of the tribe of Aser: she was of a great age, and had lived with an husband seven years from her virginity; And she was a widow of about fourscore and four years, which departed not from the temple, but served God with fastings and prayers night and day. And she coming in that instant gave thanks likewise unto the Lord, and spake of him to all them that looked for redemption in Jerusalem. And when they had performed all things according to the law of the Lord, they returned into Galilee, to their own city Nazareth.[6]

Now when Jesus was born in Bethlehem of Judaea in the days of Herod the king, behold, there came wise men from the east to Jerusalem, Saying, *Where is he that is born King of the Jews? for we have seen his star in the east, and are come to worship him.*

When Herod the king had heard these things, he was troubled, and all Jerusalem with him.

And when he had gathered all the chief priests and scribes of the people together, he demanded of them where Christ should be born. And they said unto him, *In Bethlehem of Judaea: for thus it is written by the prophet, And thou Bethlehem, in the land of Juda, art not the least among the princes of Juda: for out of thee shall come a Governor, that shall rule my people Israel.*

Then Herod, when he had privily called the wise men, enquired of them diligently what time the star appeared. And he sent them to Bethlehem, and said, `Go and search diligently for the young child; and when ye have found him, bring me word again, that I may come and worship him also.`

When they had heard the king, they departed; and, lo, the star, which they saw in the east, went before them, till it came and stood over where the young Child was. When they saw the star, they rejoiced with exceeding great joy. And when they were come into the house, they saw the young Child with Mary his mother, and fell down, and worshipped him: and when they had opened their treasures, they presented unto him gifts; gold, and frankincense, and myrrh.

And being warned of God in a dream that they should not return to Herod, they departed into their own country another way. And when they were departed, behold, the angel of the Lord appeareth to Joseph in a dream, saying,

> Arise, and take the young child and his mother, and flee into Egypt, and be thou there until I bring thee word: for Herod will seek the young child to destroy him.

When he arose, he took the young child and his mother by night, and departed into Egypt: And was there until the death of Herod: that it might be fulfilled which was spoken of the Lord by the prophet, saying,

> Out of Egypt have I called my son.

Then Herod, when he saw that he was mocked of the wise men, was exceeding wroth, and sent forth, and slew all the children that were in Bethlehem, and in all the coasts thereof, from two years old and under, according to the time which he had diligently enquired of the wise men. Then was fulfilled that which was spoken by Jeremy the prophet, saying,

> *In Rama was there a voice heard, lamentation, and weeping, and great mourning, Rachel weeping for her children, and would not be comforted, because they are not.*

But when Herod was dead, behold, an angel of the Lord appeareth in a dream to Joseph in Egypt, Saying,

> Arise, and take the young child and his mother, and go into the land of Israel: for they are dead which sought the young child's life.

And he arose, and took the young child and his mother, and came into the land of Israel. But when he heard that Archelaus did reign in Judaea in the room of his father Herod, he was afraid to go thither: notwithstanding, being warned of God in a dream, he turned aside into the parts of Galilee: And he came and dwelt in a city called Nazareth: that it might be fulfilled which was spoken by the prophets, *He shall be called a Nazarene.*[7]

IN THE BEGINNING WAS THE WORD, AND the Word was with God, and the Word was God. The same was in the beginning with God. All things were made by him; and without him was not any thing made that was made. In him was life; and the life was the light of men. And the light shineth in darkness; and the darkness comprehended it not.

There was a man sent from God, whose name was John. The same came for a witness, to bear witness of the Light, that all men through him might believe. He was not that Light, but was sent to bear witness of that Light. That was the true Light, which lighteth every man that cometh into the world. He was in the world, and the world was made by him, and the world knew him not. He came unto his own, and his own received him not. But as many as received him, to them gave he power to become the sons of God, even to them that believe on his name: Which were born, not of blood, nor of the will of the flesh, nor of the will of man, but of God.

And the Word was made flesh, and dwelt among us, (and we beheld his glory, the glory as of the only begotten of the Father,) full of grace and truth. John bare witness of him, and cried, saying, This was he of whom I spake, He that cometh after me is preferred before me: for he was before me. And of his fulness have all we received, and grace for grace. For the law was given by Moses, but grace and truth came by Jesus Christ.

No man hath seen God at any time; the only begotten Son, which is in the bosom of the Father, he hath declared him. And this is the record of John, when the Jews sent priests and Levites from Jerusalem to ask him, `Who art thou?` And he confessed, and denied not; but confessed, *I am not the Christ.* And they asked him, `What then? Art thou Elias?` And he saith, *I am not.*

`Art thou that prophet?` And he answered, *No.* Then said they unto him, `Who art thou? that we may give an answer to them that sent us. What sayest thou of thyself?` He said, *I am the voice of one crying in the wilderness, Make straight the way of the Lord, as said the prophet Esaias.*

And they which were sent were of the Pharisees. And they asked him, and said unto him, Why baptizest thou then, if thou be not that Christ, nor Elias, neither that prophet?

John answered them, saying, *I baptize with water: but there standeth one among you, whom ye know not; He it is, who coming after me is preferred before me, whose shoe's latchet I am not worthy to unloose.*

These things were done in Bethabara beyond Jordan, where John was baptizing. The next day John seeth Jesus coming unto him, and saith, *Behold the Lamb of God, which taketh away the sin of the world. This is he of whom I said, After me cometh a man which is preferred before me: for he was before me. And I knew him not: but that he should be made manifest to Israel, therefore am I come baptizing with water.*

And John bare record, saying, *I saw the Spirit descending from heaven like a dove, and it abode upon him. And I knew him not: but he that sent me to baptize with water, the same said unto me, Upon whom thou shalt see the Spirit descending, and remaining on him, the same is he which baptizeth with the Holy Ghost. And I saw, and bare record that this is the Son of God.*

Again the next day after John stood, and two of his disciples; And looking upon Jesus as he walked, he saith, Behold the Lamb of God![8]

Who has believed our message? To whom has the Lord's arm been revealed? For he grew up before him as a tender plant, and as a root out of dry ground. He has no good looks or majesty. When we see him, there is no beauty that we should desire him. He was despised and rejected by men, a man of suffering and acquainted with disease.

He was despised as one from whom men hide their face; and we didn't respect him. Surely he has borne our sickness and carried our suffering; yet we considered him plagued, struck by God, and afflicted. But he was pierced for our transgressions. He was crushed for our iniquities.

The punishment that brought our peace was on him; and by his wounds we are healed. All we like sheep have gone astray. Everyone has turned to his own way; and the Lord has laid on him the iniquity of us all. He was oppressed, yet when he was afflicted he didn't open his mouth. As a lamb that is led to the slaughter, and as a sheep that before its shearers is silent, so he didn't open his mouth. He was taken away by oppression and judgement.

As for his generation, who considered that he was cut off out of the land of the living and stricken for the disobedience of my people? They made his grave with the wicked, and with a rich man in his death, although he had done no violence, nor was any deceit in his mouth. Yet it pleased the Lord to bruise him. He has caused him to suffer.

When you make his soul an offering for sin, he will see his offspring. He will prolong his days and the Lord's pleasure will prosper in his hand. After the suffering of his soul, he will see the light and be satisfied. My righteous servant will justify many by the knowledge of himself; and he will bear their iniquities. Therefore I will give him a portion with the great. He will divide the plunder with the strong, because he poured out his soul to death and was counted with the transgressors; yet he bore the sins of many and made intercession for the transgressors.⁹

AND SUCH WERE SOME OF YOU. BUT YOU were washed, but you were sanctified, but you were justified in the name of the Lord Jesus and by the Spirit of our God.¹⁰

...BUT THESE ARE WRITTEN THAT YOU may believe that Jesus is the Christ, the Son of God, and that believing you may have life in His name.¹¹

THEREFORE WE ALSO PRAY ALWAYS FOR you that our God would count you worthy of this calling, and fulfill all the good pleasure of His goodness and the work of faith with power, that the name of our Lord Jesus Christ may be glorified in you, and you in Him, according to the grace of our God and the Lord Jesus Christ.¹²

...

For unto us a Child is born, Unto us a Son is given; And the government will be upon His shoulder. And His name will be called Wonderful, Counselor, Mighty God, Everlasting Father, Prince of Peace. Of the increase of His government and peace There will be no end, Upon the throne of David and over His kingdom, To order it and establish it with judgment and justice From that time forward, even forever. The zeal of the Lord of hosts will perform this.[13]

Glory to God in the highest, And on earth peace, goodwill toward men![14]

Amen and Blessed Merry Christmas!

O Come, Let Us Adore Him

MY PRAYER FOR YOU

Exploring the different ways that Christmas has been celebrated through the ages has truly been a joyous adventure. I consider this to be a labor of love—and a lesson learned.

What I've realized is that traditions can be whatever we want them to be. Now, this can be good when it comes to treating one another with love, honor, and respect. It is marvelous when we do good deeds for one another, and even more touching when the opportunity arises to witness actions of goodwill towards others.

But as my research led me to read about the controversies, sacrifices, traumas, and atrocities people had to go through to continue to pass the good news along, I noticed something interesting. Throughout time, humanity has learned to conform to the kingdoms of this world common mind. Our thinking, language, and actions, even some of our oral traditions have been controlled by the dictates and opinions of our times via societal, cultural, and in this present day, social media influencers.

We have familial, cultural, regional, and denominational traditions and ways to celebrate the Lord and His birth. And sometimes, as individuals we miss the best question we can ask Him. *How do You want to be celebrated?* And I think I know at least part of His answer.

To love the Lord Jesus is to love His Father, and to honor His Spirit in the earth. It is to seek His Kingdom and righteousness above *and* instead of anything else. It is to be transformed in mind, will, emotions, actions, and conversation—to move beyond and completely abandon all the prejudices, judgements, and bigoted notions that we have about one another. And ourselves. It is to live as manifested sons of the Most High God.

Many years ago, the Lord gave me a song to sing during times of prayer and intercession. It's a hallmark of the life I have chosen to live. The words: *"If you love Me, love My people. Love My people, like I do."* I still know the melody of that song, and it has been a long time since I first sang it.

Oh, I cannot begin to tell you how often I have forgotten or failed to live by those words. Especially when others that I trust, or are close to hurt, misjudge or lie about me, or mistreat me in any of the other ugly ways that people do can. And I've failed to live by those words when I am one of the people He has told me to love.

But here is what I know.

This Kingdom of God thing of ours is better than anything that this earthly, sensual, and devilish world has to offer. Loving God is not connected to whether or not I celebrate Christmas like everyone else. I really demonstrate my love for Him, when I love you.

It's better to love than to hate. It is more blessed to forgive than it is to hold fast to an offense. I don't need a big toilet paper roll list of complaints and grievances about the ways that I or people of my ethnicity, country, family, or church have been overlooked or mistreated. I do not buy into the "everyone is a racist except me" mentality. The only racist I know about is Satan. And the race he hates is human.

Jesus Christ was born because it pleased His Father, and I think that is true of each and everyone of us as well. God is glad we're here on the earth. And I'll tell you what else I know: it is His pleasure to free us from every hindrance that would prohibit us from fulfilling

His dreams and plan for our lives. We just have to give up the excuses.

So, in this season of goodwill toward others, I release the healing, wholeness, soundness, love, peace, and joy that abounds in God's kingdom to you and yours. I release the will of my Father King into your lives, and pray that you grant Him the opening to become involved in every aspect of your life. I pray that He is able to make His dreams for your life come into being on earth.

As a representative of the One who was born of a virgin, looked beyond and despised the shame of the Cross because of the glorious life the Father granted Him to see, I release the blessings of Christmas in this age that has come, into your life. I call forth the particles of possibilities into active duty in your mind, will, emotions, actions, and vocabulary. I pray that as your eyes of understanding are opened, you are able to see the reality of all that God Himself caused to be spoken of you in the books that He wrote to validate your calling and election.

The oral traditions that Heaven has spoken regarding the glories of His Kingdom and will being done through your life are hereby called into remembrance. In the same manner that God prophesied and fulfilled the promise that brought Jesus Christ, the Saviour of humanity into the earth, so now the words that He has prophesied over you shall be fulfilled. His Kingdom come and will be done in the earth that is you, as Heaven has proclaimed. Because it pleases the Father to have it be so. And because you are loved eternally.

In the Name of Jesus, it is so.

Christmastime is Here!

Thank you so much for reading this book. It is my prayer that you have enjoyed the journey.

I had a lot of fun doing research. One of the things I did was to ask my Facebook friends about favorite holiday desserts. Thanks to their enthusiastic responses, we found oodles of recipes to share. You're invited to follow our:

Christmas Through The Ages
Dominion Unlimited Pinterest Board

We're loading it up with links to:
Holiday Dessert Recipes
Christmas Through The Ages Coloring Pages
Lists of Christmastime Favorites
Christmas Illustrations and Fun Facts
Vocal recording of *The Best Christmas Story Ever!*

We have gifts for you!

An audio version of *The Best Christmas Story Ever!* read by Pastor Lonzine Lee available on Spotify, YouTube, and Pinterest.

A free download of *The Best Christmas Story Ever!* is available on our website.

You'll find the audio links and the PDF at: www.dominionunlimited.org *after* December 20, 2024.

After all, it is a Christmas gift.

References & Resources

THE FIRST NOEL

1. The word we refer to as *Christmas* originates from the Old English term *Cristes maesse*. Referring to the celebration as a mass or liturgical service that was dedicated to Jesus Christ. Oxford English Dictionary, 2nd ed., s.v. "Christmas" (Oxford: Oxford University Press, 1989).
2. Sandys, William. *Christmas Carols, Ancient and Modern.* London: Richard Beckley, 1823.

   Harper, Douglas. "Noel." Online Etymology Dictionary. Accessed November 22, 2024. https://www.etymonline.com/word/noel.

   Nissenbaum, Stephen. *The Battle for Christmas.* New York: Knopf, 1996.

   Stainer, John, ed. *Christmas Carols, New and Old.* London: Novello, Ewer & Co., 1871.

GO, TELL IT ON THE MOUNTAIN

1. Ecclesiastes 1:4, 9-11 NKJV
2. Paul Andrew Moore, *Thy Kingdom Come: The Historical, Cultural, and Practical Perspective of Kingdom Theology* (Digital Publishing of Florida, Incorporated, 2022). https//www.amazon.com/Thy-Kingdom-Come-Historical-Perspective/dp/1956793593. Chapter 13, Pg. 354.

3. The New Testament writings speak of the things heard in several places. See 1 Thessalonians 2:13, Hebrews 2:1, 3; James 5:11, 1 John 1:1-5, 3:11; 2 John 1:6 for examples.
4. John Wesley Work, Jr., *New Jubilee Songs and Folk Songs of the American Negro* (1907).
5. Videos
    Go Tell It On The Mountain: Lyrics Video. Available at: https://youtu.be/YO8CW01aklU
    The Story Behind Go Tell It On The Mountain. Available at: https://youtu.be/PGOcASwtv8c
    Websites
    The Berean Test: A detailed analysis of the song's lyrics and message. Available at: https://www.thebereantest.com/john-wesley-work-jr-go-tell-it-on-the-mountain
    Hymncharts: Insight into the story behind the carol. Available at: https://www.hymncharts.com/2023/11/21/the-story-behind-go-tell-it-on-the-mountain/
    Wikipedia: Background on Go Tell It On The Mountain. Available at: https://en.wikipedia.org/wiki/Go_Tell_It_on_the_Mountain_(song)
    Wikipedia: Biography of John Wesley Work, Jr. Available at: https://en.wikipedia.org/wiki/John_Wesley_Work_Jr.
    Gaither More Than Music. *Go Tell It On The Mountain: The Story Behind the Song.* https://gaither.com/go-tell-it-on-the-mountain-the-story-behind-the-song/

A THRILL OF HOPE

1. Tertullian, *On the Flesh of Christ* (c. 206 CE)
2. As described in Hippolytus of Rome, *Commentary on Daniel*, c. 202 CE.

REFERENCES & RESOURCES

3. Early Christian Writings (http://www.earlychristianwritings.com/hippolytus.html): Features translations of Hippolytus' key works, often with academic commentary, although his works are often fragmentary.
   You can access the full sermon here. It's a very interesting read. Hippolytus of Rome, *Commentary on Daniel*, trans. T.C. Schmidt, Book 4, Section 23.3, accessed November 6, 2024, https://www.pergrazia.com/wp-content/uploads/2019/12/0205_hippolytus_commentary-on-daniel_2010.pdf.
4. "Church Fathers on Christmas: John Chrysostom." *1517*. Accessed November 22, 2024. https://www.1517.org/articles/church-fathers-on-christmas-john-chrysostom.
5. "But to you who fear My name The Sun of Righteousness shall arise with healing in His wings; And you shall go out and grow fat like stall-fed calves." Malachi 4:2 NKJV
6. Digital Medievalist. "The Calendar of 354." Accessed November 21, 2024. https://www.digitalmedievalist.com/things/manuscripts/the-calendar-of-354/.
   General Overview from Wikipedia:
   Wikipedia contributors. "Chronograph of 354." Last modified November 20, 2024. https://en.wikipedia.org/wiki/Chronograph_of_354.
7. [1] Hippolytus of Rome, *Commentary on Daniel*, c. 202 CE.
   [2] John Chrysostom, *Homily on the Nativity of Christ*, c. 386 CE.
   [3] Augustine of Hippo, *Sermon 192* in *The Works of Saint Augustine: A Translation for the 21st Century*, Vol. III, Sermons 148-183, ed. John E. Rotelle (Hyde Park, NY: New City Press, 1992).

MARY, DID YOU KNOW?

1. συμβάλλω (symballō). Theological Dictionary of the New Testament. Grand Rapids: Eerdmans, 1964–1976.
2. Renner, Rick. Sparkling Gems from the Greek, Volume 1. Tulsa: Teach All Nations, 2003. Entry for January 1st. Accessed November 18, 2024. [https://renner.org/wp-content/uploads/2013/11/sparkling-gems-excerpt.pdf] (https://renner.org/wp-content/uploads/2013/11/sparkling-gems-excerpt.pdf).
3. Mounce, William D. "συμβάλλω." Greek Dictionary. Accessed November 18, 2024. [https://www.billmounce.com/greek-dictionary/symballo] (https://www.billmounce.com/greek-dictionary/symballo).
4. Luke 2:41-52 KJV
5. "διατηρέω." Theological Dictionary of the New Testament. Grand Rapids: Eerdmans, 1964–1976.
6. Blue Letter Bible. "Greek Lexicon: διατηρέω (diatēreō)." Accessed November 18, 2024. [https://www.blueletterbible.org/lexicon/g1301/] (https://www.blueletterbible.org/lexicon/g1301/).
   Mounce, William D. "διατηρέω." Greek Dictionary. Accessed November 18, 2024. [https://www.billmounce.com/greek-dictionary/diatereo] (https://www.billmounce.com/greek-dictionary/diatereo).

O TANNENBAUM

1. "Glass Christmas Ornaments," *The German Way & More*, accessed November 28, 2024, https://www.german-way.com/history-and-culture/holidays-and-celebrations/christmas/glass-christmas-ornaments.
   "Christmas Ornament," *Wikipedia*, last modified

November 25, 2024, https://en.wikipedia.org/wiki/Christmas_ornament.
2. "The History of Christmas Ornaments, Part 2," *Ornament Shop*, accessed November 28, 2024, https://www.ornamentshop.com/pages/history-story-part2.

"Shiny Brite Ornaments: Valuable, Nostalgic Christmas Baubles," *Do You Remember?*, accessed November 28, 2024, https://doyouremember.com/54902/shiny-brite-ornaments-valuable-nostalgic-christmas-baubles.

3. Jeremiah 10:1-5 NET. For greater context, it is good to understand that Jeremiah was speaking with regard to idolatry. Theologians and scholars believe the reference concerning silver and gold speaks to cutting down a tree, bringing the wood into the home/work area, carving an idol, then covering it in those metals to worship.

If you're really interested in learning a bit more, the following references might be of interest to you.

Feinberg, Charles L. "Jeremiah." In *The Expositor's Bible Commentary*, edited by Frank E. Gaebelein, Vol. 6, 395–398. Grand Rapids, MI: Zondervan, 1986. This section provides commentary on Jeremiah 10, emphasizing the prophet's denunciation of idol worship.

Thompson, J.A. *The Book of Jeremiah*. The New International Commentary on the Old Testament. Grand Rapids, MI: William B. Eerdmans Publishing Company, 1980. See pages 316–320 for an in-depth analysis of Jeremiah 10:1–16, focusing on the critique of idolatry.

Harris, R. Laird, Gleason L. Archer Jr., and Bruce K. Waltke, eds. *Theological Wordbook of the Old Testament*. Chicago: Moody Press, 1980. See entries for "עֵץ" (*ēṣ*, "tree") and "פֶּסֶל" (*pesel*, "idol") for detailed discussions relevant to Jeremiah 10.

4. Theological Wordbook of the Old Testament (TWOT): Harris, R. Laird, Gleason L. Archer Jr., and Bruce K. Waltke, eds. *Theological Wordbook of the Old Testament.* Chicago: Moody Press, 1980. See entries for "עֵץ" (ʿēṣ, "tree") and "פֶּסֶל" (*pesel*, "idol") for detailed discussions relevant to Jeremiah 10.

    Thompson, J.A. *The Book of Jeremiah.* The New International Commentary on the Old Testament. Grand Rapids, MI: William B. Eerdmans Publishing Company, 1980. See pages 316–320 for an in-depth analysis of Jeremiah 10:1–16, focusing on the critique of idolatry.

5. Jeremiah 10:6-12 NET
6. History Channel. "The History of the Christmas Tree." Last modified December 2023. https://www.history.com/topics/christmas/history-of-christmas-trees.

    EWTN. "The Christmas Tree: Legends, Traditions, History." Accessed November 2024. https://www.ewtn.com/catholicism/library/christmas-tree-legends-traditions-history-1763.

7. **Germany**: By the 16th century, fir trees were adorned with apples (symbolizing the forbidden fruit), nuts, and paper roses.

    Scandinavia: Incorporated the tree into Yule traditions. Candles and straw ornaments were adapted in Nordic countries to honor light and life in the harsh winters.

    United Kingdom: Queen Victoria and Prince Albert popularized the Christmas tree in the 19th century, a blend of German traditions and British festivity.

    Mexico: Maintains traditional *Nacimiento* (nativity scenes), and blended Catholic and local customs with the adoption of Christmas trees.

    Japan: Trees are sometimes adorned with origami

cranes and other local crafts as part of a secular celebration.

USA: In the 18th century, German immigrants introduced the Christmas tree, which became a central symbol of American Christmas celebrations by the 19th century.

8. You can compare the differences in the German and English translations on this site.

> Vesty, Amanda C. "O Christmas Tree! History of the Traditional O Tannenbaum Christmas 'Carol.'" Last modified December 10, 2020. O Christmas Tree! History of the traditional O Tannenbaum Christmas Carol.

If you're interested in reading a bit more about this Carol's traditions, the following resources may prove helpful.

> Keller, Peter. "The Evolution of 'O Tannenbaum': From Folk Song to Christmas Classic." *Music and Cultural Heritage Quarterly* 28, no. 2 (2019): 102–112.
>
> Wright, Lydia. "Fir Trees and Festivities: The Global Spread of 'O Christmas Tree.'" *Journal of Holiday Traditions* 14, no. 1 (2016): 45–58.

NOT A CREATURE WAS STIRRING

1. Davies, Owen, *Paganism: A Very Short Introduction.* Oxford: Oxford University Press, 2011.

   > Wikipedia contributors. "Paganism." Wikipedia. https://en.wikipedia.org/wiki/Paganism#cite_note-Bowersock1999p625-1. Accessed November 22, 2024.

2. "Santa Claus History." *History Skills.* https://www.historyskills.com/classroom/year-8/santa-claus-history/. Accessed November 22, 2024.

   > "Who is St. Nicholas? The Origin of Santa Claus." *St. Nicholas Center.* https://www.stnicholascenter.org/

who-is-st-nicholas/origin-of-santa. Accessed November 22, 2024.

"How Did St. Nicholas Become Santa Claus?" *Ancient Pages*. https://www.ancientpages.com/2023/12/22/how-did-st-nicholas-become-santa-claus/. Accessed November 22, 2024.

3. Washington Irving. *Knickerbocker's History of New York*. Project Gutenberg. Book II, Chapter V. https://www.gutenberg.org/files/13042/13042-h/13042-h.htm. Accessed November 22, 2024.
4. Check out this fun little animated story. Louis Armstrong, "'Twas The Night Before Christmas (Official Animated Video)," YouTube, November 3, 2022, https://youtu.be/cmt2TZWGoO8.
5. There are two versions of this poem. The most famous one, *A Visit From St. Nicholas* is attributed to Clement Clarke Moore. The second version, entitled: *Account Of A Visit From St. Nicholas* is by Major Henry Livingston, Jr.. Both poems can be accessed on *The Poetry Foundation* website:

     A Visit from St. Nicholas | The Poetry Foundation
     Account of a Visit From St. Nicholas: Second version by Major Henry Livingston, Jr.

HARK! HEAR THE BELLS

1. Henry Wadsworth Longfellow, *The Complete Poetical Works of Henry Wadsworth Longfellow* (Boston: Houghton Mifflin, 1893), 479. Accessed December 1, 2024. https://archive.org/details/completepoetical1922long.

    Justin Taylor, "The True Story Behind 'I Heard the Bells on Christmas Day,'" The Gospel Coalition, December 21, 2014, https://www.thegospelcoalition.org/blogs/justin-taylor/the-story-of-pain-and-hope-behind-i-heard-the-bells-on-christmas-day/.

REFERENCES & RESOURCES

"I Heard the Bells on Christmas Day (Civil War background)," video, YouTube, https://youtu.be/oZtNlZmnEMU?si=ET7KUUGhxaHDxt3B.

Wikipedia, s.v. "I Heard the Bells on Christmas Day," accessed November 2024, https://en.wikipedia.org/wiki/I_Heard_the_Bells_on_Christmas_Day.

Casting Crowns, "I Heard the Bells on Christmas Day (Yule Log)," video, YouTube, https://youtu.be/haaes9anfvs?si=Sm1ZHVx25xWCAGa_.

CeCe Winans, "I Heard The Bells On Christmas Day, Live Performance at Belmont Christmas," video, YouTube, https://youtu.be/7d9q8BcVrRU?si=wO82yYBRYszOqxO5.

2. Carol of the Bells - Ukrainian Bell Carol, performed by Belsnickel Records, YouTube video, 3:56, December 12, 2017, [https://youtu.be/hCXyg6HkuDo] (https://youtu.be/hCXyg6HkuDo).

Carol of the Bells https://en.wikipedia.org/wiki/Shchedryk_(song)

100th Premiere Anniversary of Shchedryk in New York

https://youtu.be/hCXyg6HkuDo?si=6i0NDTMIaYSfQza7

Shchedryk / Щедрик. Carol of the Bells. Original Ukrainian Version with English and Ukrainian Lyrics - https://www.youtube.com/watch?v=GqeJ38DThVc

Tina Karol – Shchedryk Lyric Translate (for lyrics and translations): https://lyricstranslate.com

3. Bell Science Resources

Strike Tone," Wikipedia, last modified November 1, 2024, https://en.wikipedia.org/wiki/Strike_tone.

What Is a Strike Tone?" National Bell Festival, accessed December 1, 2024, https://www.bells.org/blog/what-is-bell-strike-tone.

Bart Hopkin, "Fundamental, Harmonics, Overtones, Partials, Modes," Bart Hopkin Musical

Innovations, accessed December 1, 2024, https://barthopkin.com/fundamental-harmonics-overtones-partials-modes/.

Additional Reference:

James Blades, Percussion Instruments and Their History (London: Faber and Faber, 2005). Accessed December 1, 2024. https://archive.org/details/percussioninstru00jame.

Trevor Cox, The Sound Book: The Science of the Sonic Wonders of the World (New York: W.W. Norton & Company, 2014). Accessed December 1, 2024. https://wwnorton.com/books/The-Sound-Book/.

I HAVE A LITTLE DREIDEL

1. *A tractate is like a chapter or volume in a larger legal and theological encyclopedia, focusing on one specific subject area within Jewish law and tradition.*
2. "What Is the Talmud?" *Chabad.org*. Accessed November 29, 2024. https://www.chabad.org/library/article_cdo/aid/3347866/jewish/What-Is-the-Talmud.htm.

   "Talmud and Midrash." *Encyclopaedia Britannica*. Accessed November 29, 2024. https://www.britannica.com/topic/Talmud.
3. For the full text of the account of Eleazar the Scribe's choice to stand in the face of persecution faced by Jews under Antiochus IV Epiphanes you can refer to the Douay-Rheims online edition on Bible Gateway: 2 Maccabees 6:18–31: 2 Maccabees 6:18–31." *Douay-Rheims 1899 American Edition*. Bible Gateway. Accessed November 29, 2024. https://www.biblegateway.com/passage/?search=2+Maccabees+6%3A18-31&version=DRA.
4. 1 Maccabees 1:10–64 describes the rise of Antiochus IV, his desecration of the Temple, and the resulting

persecution of the Jewish people. 2 Maccabees 6–7 recounts specific acts of resistance, including the martyrdom of Eleazar and the story of Chanah and her seven sons.

1 Maccabees 1:10–64: https://www.biblegateway.com/passage/?search=1+Maccabees+1%3A10-64&version=NRSVUE

2 Maccabees 6–7: https://www.biblegateway.com/passage/?search=2+Maccabees+6-7&version=NRSVUE

The detailed account of Chanah and her seven sons can be accessed on the BibleGateway.com site.

2 Maccabees 7: *Bible Gateway*. Accessed November 29, 2024. https://www.biblegateway.com/passage/?search=2+Maccabees+7&version=RSV.

4 Maccabees 8–18: *Bible Gateway*. Accessed November 29, 2024. https://www.biblegateway.com/passage/?search=4+Maccabees+8&version=CEB.

If you're interested in reading more of the Apocrypha online, here are to options to choose from.

Common English Bible. *Bible Gateway*. Accessed November 29, 2024. https://www.biblegateway.com/versions/Common-English-Bible-CEB/.

Douay-Rheims 1899 American Edition. *Bible Gateway*. Accessed November 29, 2024. https://www.biblegateway.com/versions/Douay-Rheims-1899-American-Edition-DRA-Bible/.

5. "Hanukkah 2023: Stories, Traditions & Origins." *History.com*. November 27, 2023. https://www.history.com/topics/holidays/hanukkah.

"The Story of Dreidel." *Chabad.org/Kids*. Accessed November 28, 2024. https://www.chabad.org/kids/article_cdo/aid/368225/jewish/The-Story-of-Dreidel.htm.

"Hershel and the Hanukkah Goblins (25th

Anniversary Edition)." *Amazon.* Accessed November 28, 2024. Hershel and the Hanukkah Goblins.

If you prefer to listen to this story, you can do so on YouTube. Hershel and the Hanukkah Goblins. *YouTube.* Published December 8, 2020. Accessed November 29, 2024. https://www.youtube.com/watch?v=4UnYCmasvEs.

Fischer, Ellen. *Latke, the Lucky Dog.* Kar-Ben Publishing, 2014.

Adler, David A. *The Story of Hanukkah.* Holiday House, 2011.

Kimmel, Eric A. *Hanukkah Bear.* Holiday House, 2013.

Simon, Tanya, and Richard Simon. *Oskar and the Eight Blessings.* Roaring Brook Press, 2015.

Other resources related to the Dreidel game and song:

"How to Play Dreidel." *Chabad.org.* Accessed November 29, 2024. https://www.chabad.org/holidays/chanukah/article_cdo/aid/597253/jewish/How-to-Play-Dreidel.htm.

"Dreidel Song - I Have a Little Dreidel." *Chabad.org.* Accessed November 29, 2024. https://www.chabad.org/multimedia/music_cdo/aid/797123/jewish/Dreidel-Song.htm.

"I Have A Little Dreidel - Animated Version." *YouTube.* Published November 28, 2023. Accessed November 29, 2024. https://www.youtube.com/watch?v=Pg6oiqyIqNo.

6. Cindye Coates, *The Fulfilled Prophecies of Jesus: A Verse-By-Verse Study of Matthew 24* (Atlanta, GA: Present Truth Publishers, 2022). Available on Amazon: https://a.co/d/1POQUiS.

Present Truth Matters, Podcast hosted by Dr. Cindye Coates. Accessed November 28, 2024. www.PresentTruthMatters.com.

TROLL THE ANCIENT YULETIDE CAROL

1. Bede, Venerable. *The Reckoning of Time.* Translated by Faith Wallis. Liverpool: Liverpool University Press, 1999.
   Roll, Susan K. *Toward the Origins of Christmas.* Kampen: Kok Pharos, 1995.
   Deacy, Christopher, and G. A. D. Draper, eds. *Theology and Christmas: Essays on the History and Tradition of Yuletide.* Oxford: Oxford University Press, 2008.
2. Fletcher, Richard. *The Barbarian Conversion: From Paganism to Christianity.* New York: Henry Holt and Company, 1997.
   Wallace-Hadrill, J. M. *The Frankish Church.* Oxford: Clarendon Press, 1983.
   Yorke, Barbara. *The Conversion of Britain: Religion, Politics and Society in Britain c. 600-800.* London: Pearson Education Limited, 2006.
3. "What Is 'Yuletide', Anyway?" *History Things,* September 14, 2023. Accessed November 21, 2024. https://historythings.com/what-is-yuletide-anyway/.

'TWAS THE BIRTHDAY OF A KING

1. Luke 1:1-80 NAS95
2. John 3:16-17
3. Isaiah 9:1-2
4. Isaiah 9:6-7
5. Matthew 1:18-25
6. Luke 2:1-39
7. Matthew 2:1-23 KJV
8. John 1:1-36 KJV
9. Isaiah 53:1-12 WMBBE

10. 1 Corinthians 6:11
11. John 20:31
12. 2 Thessalonians 1:11-12
13. Isaiah 9:2,6-7
14. Luke 2:14

About the Author

Lonzine Lee is a pastor, prophetic teacher, writer, worshipper, songwriter, editorial consultant, and aspiring voiceover talent. She writes for the edification of the Body of Christ and seekers of the Kingdom of God, and works with other authors to do the same thing.

She is currently at work on a series of books and study guides compatible with her first book, *Kingdom 101: The Supernatural Reality of Heaven on Earth*. Every book she writes is designed to help you gain a firm foundation in the teachings and life in the Kingdom of God.

Pastor Lonzine, also known as PL3 to her Astounding Love family, is passionate about motivating others to seek and live the Kingdom life and to know Christ's love and perfection.

Pastor Lonzine honestly believes that the Kingdom of God is the place where you discover and realize the dreams that God has for you. You can trust Him to make His dreams come true. She is a fervent believer that fulfilling your Kingdom destiny manifests healing to the nations. She plans to release *Our Quest For Identity,* the first book in the Kingdom 101 Foundations series in December 2024. She also invites you to stay tuned for news about *Spirit Warrior,* her first fiction novella.

You can learn more about the ministry at www.astoundinglove.org or visit her website, www.dominionunlimited.org.

Watch Lonzine teach, and talk with others about the Kingdom of God Life. Her broadcast
Kingdom Conversations With Lonzine Lee
and
a variety of Kingdom of God teachings can be found on the **Dominion Unlimited YouTube** page.

youtube.com/@DomUnltdMsElle3
linkedin.com/in/lonzine-lee-mba-5392429
pinterest.com/dominionunlimited

Also by Lonzine Lee

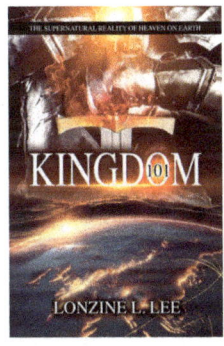

Available on Amazon.com

Kingdom 101: The Supernatural Reality of Heaven on Earth

liance

www.ingramcontent.com/pod-product-compliance
Lightning Source LLC
Chambersburg PA
CBHW062003180426
43198CB00036B/2149